THE DARK MOON

SHADES OF EQUALITY:
UNMASKING COLOR DISCRIMINATION

KAHKASHAN ZAID

BLUEROSE PUBLISHERS
India | U.K.

Copyright © Kahkashan Zaid 2023

All rights reserved by author. No part of this publication may be reproduced, stored in a retrieval system or transmitted in any form or by any means, electronic, mechanical, photocopying, recording or otherwise, without the prior permission of the author. Although every precaution has been taken to verify the accuracy of the information contained herein, the publisher assumes no responsibility for any errors or omissions. No liability is assumed for damages that may result from the use of information contained within.

BlueRose Publishers takes no responsibility for any damages, losses, or liabilities that may arise from the use or misuse of the information, products, or services provided in this publication.

For permissions requests or inquiries regarding this publication, please contact:

BLUEROSE PUBLISHERS
www.BlueRoseONE.com
info@bluerosepublishers.com
+91 8882 898 898
+4407342408967

ISBN: 978-93-5819-124-0

Cover design: Muskan Sachdeva
Typesetting: Rohit

First Edition: August 2023

We all know, that humans have a lotof deficiency, everybody has a different kind of mindset, but I feel sorry for those, who think, that color is a massive deficiency in a human, it doesn't matter, is a man or a woman, but most of the time, they target women.

Society always targets black woman and says a lot of things, like, "Hey man, her complexion is black, now what will happen to her, now who will marry her "etc.

And the fun fact is that her parents said the line first. We need to understand that, babies don't know about color, you put in them, that, black color is the worst color, you don't look gorgeous in it, you look ugly.

Parents should teach their children that, color is not a character, but your character, make your color beautiful.

When I was in school, one of my classmates was so beautiful, her smile, her heart, and her words, but she always complain God that, why he gave me this complexion, and she always used to come to my seat and tell me, how fair is your skin, and how dark is my complexion, Why did God make me like this, I never laughed at her, but I used to get very bored, but After some time, I realized that, society is not accept a beautiful woman on black complexion. This is a very harsh truth. If a colour can decide your destiny, then a fair complexion have the most beautiful destiny, but we all know this is not the truth.

But Now in this Era is very confident, and they accept themselves, they are not ashamed of themselves. But there is a certain amount of people, who still think that, color is a deficiency.

I always thought this is an Indian society's problem, but I was wrong, this problem is all over the world.

The story is about complexion, not just black but a fair.

Outside the labour room. Viraj waiting for his newborn baby, his brother Ganesh, giving him a courage:

Ganesh : Brother, everything will be all right.

Viraj : Hmmm.

Doctor came:

Viraj : Doctor, my wife?

Doctor : congratulations, your wife gave birth to a baby girl.

Viraj and Ganesh are very:

Viraj : And my wife, Saanvi?

Doctor : She is fine.

Viraj : Shall we meet?

Doctor : Wait for a minute, when we shift in general ward, then you can meet.

Viraj : Ok, thank you Doctor.

Doctor : It's ok.

    Doctor left from there. After some time, Viraj and Ganesh goes to meet, Saanvi and Viraj's daughter.

Ganesh : congratulations, sister in law.

Saanvi : Thank you.

    When Viraj and Ganesh saw a baby, they shock:

The Dark Moon

Ganesh : Brother, she is so dark.

    When they heard this line, Viraj and Saanvi looking at each other.

    2 years of Chandni, she plays with her toys. Ganesh came up:

Ganesh : hey darky.

    And he left from there. Saanvi said while being upset:

Saanvi : what will happen to her?

Viraj : don't know.

    8 years of Chandni:

    Society started telling Saanvi and Viraj:

    Saanvi and Chandni coming from the market, their neighbor Aunty Divya:

Divya : Saanvi, your daughter is so dark, do something for her? Who will marry her?

    Saanvi got upset and she came up her home. Viraj asks Saanvi:

Viraj : what happen saanvi? Why are you upset?

    Saanvi starts crying:

Saanvi : why our daughter is so Black, everyone is telling us, that our daughter is so dark.

    Chandni got hurt by this line, and she has tears in her eyes. She goes to her room and start crying very badly.

    Divya always tries to give her a bad feeling that her color is so dark, and her parents said that to her, that her color is not beautiful, cryalways crying.

Chandni starts to feel insecure with her complexion.

whenever she passed by Divya's house, Divya asks her:

Divya : hey darky? How are you?

Chandni never said anything, she was always silent and left from there.

Divya : God knows what will happen with her, this is not my concern.

Chandni used to get upset with Divya's words.

After a few years, in school, Chandni is seating alone, and her classmates call her, "Darky"

Ananya her classmate, come up with her friends:

Ananya : Hey Darky, you literally have this black color or have you applied charcoal on your body, because your color is so black.

They are laughing at her, and Chandni is crying. She came to her house from her school, she Is crying and furious, her father asks her:

Viraj : What happened my child? Why are you crying?

Chandni : Why my name is Chandni, I am not like moon, my color is not like moon, my face is

The Dark Moon

> not bright as moon, then why my name is Chandni?

Viraj is smiling, And says very politely :

Viraj : It's ok my child.

> He left from there, Chandni is very angry on Viraj's words, she said to herself in her mind:

Chandni : Nothing is ok dad.

> Next day, in school. Teacher is teaching. principal came up with Albinism girl Chhaiya, everyone is watching her.

The whole class together: Good morning ma'am.

Principal : Good morning class, how are you all of you?

Class : all good.

Principal : excellent, meet Chhaiya, you're New classmate.

Ananya : wow....., there is a black girl name Chandni in our class, now a white girl name Chhaiya is coming.

> The whole class is laughing at them, Chandni got upset, but Chhaiya smiles with them.

Teacher : Ananya, shut up.

Ananya : sorry ma'am .

Principal : Chhaiya? Where do you want to sit?

> Chhaiya sees the whole class, she saw Chandni, she was smiling.

Chhaiya : I want to sit there.

Principal : With Chandni?

Chhaiya : yes ma'am.

Principal : Then go and sit over there.

> Chhaiya goes to sit with Chandni. The principal left from there.

Recess Time :

> Ananya came up to Chandni and Chhaiya's bench:

Ananya : Hey black and white, how are you both? By the way, you both going to be best friend, you know why? Ask me why.

Chhaiya : We don't want to know?

> Ananya got angry, but she says with smile:

Ananya : Because black and white is always match.

> Chhaiya comes to her Swag:

Chhaiya : I think you are right, but I am not going to say anything wrong, because this is my first day of school, I do not want to be suspended, so please, give us some peace, Okay....?

Ananya got angry again:

Ananya : What did you say?

Chhaiya : If we are black and white, then you are deaf, I am not going to repeat, understood?

> Ananya attacks Chhaiya with a bag on her back. Chhaiya controls herself and says very politely:

Chhaiya : Have you calmed down or do you want to beat me more?

The Dark Moon

             Ananya got more furious, she was going to do again but her friends stopped her.

Ananya : You do not know me.

Chhaiya : I do not have cheap interest, guys, please take your friend from here.

Ananya : I will see you.

Chhaiya : Of course.

             Ananya and her friends left from there. Chandni is nervous, she is looking Chhaiya, Chhaiya very politely says to Chandni:

Chhaiya : Why are you staring me like this?

Chandni : Nothing.

Chhaiya : Are you afraid of me?

             Chandni is nervous :

Chandni : Nope.

Chhaiya : Do not afraid of me, I am your friend, and you are my best friend.

Chandni : What! How can we be friend?

Chhaiya : Why? We can not be friend?

Chandni : Why not, but we meet today!

Chhaiya : You are the first girl, who sit next to me, who don't tell me that, don't sit with me.

Chandni : And you are the first girl, who want to sit next to me, before you, nobody sit next to me.

Chhaiya's hand towards Chandni :

Chhaiya : Friends?

Chandni : Nope….., best friends.

Both shake hands.

Both share their tiffin box, both playing with each other, hangout with each other.

After few days. In class room :

Ananya : Hey black and white? How are you both?

Chhaiya : We are excellent deaf.

Ananya got angry :

Ananya : Mind your tongue.

Chhaiya : Apply that yourself first.

Ananya : Don't you think that, you are such a out spoken person?

Chhaiya : Don't you think that, you are such a out spoken person?

Ananya : Don't repeat my words.

Chhaiya : Then, don't tease me.

Chandni : Please shut your mouth Chhaiya.

Ananya : You are right Darky, you should teach your friend, how to behave with me.

Chandni : She doesn't need to learn how to behave with someone, you should learn how to behave with others.

Ananya got furious, and slap Chandni.

Ananya : Mind your tongue Darky.

Chhaiya attacks Ananya with bag on her face. The fight began

Principal office. Ananya, Chandni and Chhaiya stand in front of principal.

The Dark Moon

Principal : What you guys did, this is a school, I not a Fight Club.

Ananya : Ma'am, they started fighting.

Chhaiya : No ma'am, she is lying.

Principal : Shut up both of you.

Chandni : Don't listen to us, you should check CCTV footage, you will know better.

Principal watching CCTV footage.

Principal : Chhaiya and Chandni, please go to your class.

Both together : Thank you, ma'am.

Both left from there.

Chhaiya : We are safe because of you.

Chandni : But Ananya is not.

They both start laughing.

Principal angrily :

Principal : Ananya, I am going to call your parents right now, and you are suspended from school for a week.

Ananya : Ma'am please sorry, please don't call my parents, I will not do again, please don't suspend me, please ma'am? Please...

Principal : Nope, you made a mistake, you have to punish.

Ananya : Please ma'am, don't call my parents.

Principal : For a condition.

Ananya : Yes ma'am, whatever the condition, I will fulfill it.

Kahkashan Zaid

>Ananya is stand under the sunlight:
>
>After the all classes. Chhaiya and Chandni came up to Ananya :

Chhaiya : Hey Ananya, how are you?

Ananya : You both Would be very happy?

Chandni : You always mistake here, we did not anything, you started misbehave with us, you started fighting, we did not, you never accept your mistakes, that's why you are here.

Chhaiya : let it be, she deserves.

>Both left from there, Ananya got furious.
>
>After few years :
>
>Chandni came up to Chhaiya's house:

Chandni : Good morning Uncle & Aunty?

Both together : Good morning.

Vinod : How are you Chandni?

Chandni : I am excellent.

Seema : Excited for the first day of degree college?

Chandni : I am nervous more than excited.

>Both understand her words.

Chandni : where is Chhaiya Please call her, we are getting late for college.

Seema : Okay.

>Meanwhile, Chhaiya came :

Chhaiya : Hey Chandni.

Chandni : Hey.

The Dark Moon

Chhaiya : Let's go, bye mom dad.

Chandni : Bye uncle auntie.

Both together : bye.

Both left from there.

Vinod : Both are different, in a nature, in a complexion, but they are still friends.

Seema : Friend wants friend, nothing else.

Chandni and Chhaiya sat in a Taxi, Chandni is silent, Chhaiya asks Chandni:

Chhaiya : Chandni? Chandni?

Chandni : Yes.

Chhaiya : What happened?

Chandni : What happened?

Chhaiya : Are you nervous?

Chandni : Hmmmm, Don't you feel bad, when everyone calls us black and white?

Chhaiya : We are black and white, so what? Do you feel bad?

Chandni : Of course, I feel bad, you are an Albinism girl, no one point to you, but I have a black complexion, and everyone laughs at me, because I am so dark.

Chhaiya says nothing. Both arrive in college, whoever sees them, they are laughing at them, Chhaiya is smiling, and Chandni feels ashamed. Chandni Asks Chhaiya:

Chandni : Why are you smiling? Everyone is laughing at us.

~ 11 ~

Chhaiya : You smile too.

Chandni : What!

Chhaiya : Smile.

Chandni also smiles. Both arrive in class:

Chandni : Why you told me to do smile?

Chhaiya : If we didn't smile, they would have laughed more at us, class is about to start.

The class starts.

Chhaiya came up her home :

Chhaiya : Hey Mom.

Seema : Hey, how was your day?

Chhaiya : Phenomenal.

Seema : good.

Chandni came up to her home, she is very upset :

Saanvi : Chandni?

Chandni : Yes Mom?

Saanvi : Why are you upset?

Chandni : Nothing.

Saanvi : You did not have a good day in college?

She started crying :

Saanvi : Are you crying? Why are you crying?

Chandni : Why God gave me this complexion? I am ugly.

Saanvi : You are not ugly my child.

Chandni : No, I am ugly, you both gave me this feeling, that I am ugly, you both never said to me

The Dark Moon

that, I am beautiful, you both always said to me, that what will happen to me, is my fault, that I have dark complexion? why people don't understand, that this is just a color, nothing else?

Chandni goes to her room. Saanvi's eyes get wet.

In college, students started teasing both of them, they call them black and white. Chhaiya never effected by all of this, but Chandni get anxious and depressed. She always complains God And cried in her room.

On the dinning table, everyone does dinner together, Chandni is upset, eating slowly:

Viraj : Chandni? Chandni?

Chandni : Yes dad?

Viraj : Why are you not eating properly?

Chandni : I am eating dad.

Viraj : Are you upset?

Chandni got angry :

Chandni : You don't need to worry about it.

Saanvi : Chandni! What kind of accent are you using in front of your dad!

Chandni : Why….! Let it be, I don't want to talk to you both.

Chandni was about to go, Saanvi slap her, Chandni left from there.

Viraj : Why did you do that?

Kahkashan Zaid

Saanvi : She needed.

    Next day, Chhaiya came up to Chandni's home :

Chhaiya : Hello Aunty, Good morning.

Saanvi : Hello dear, Good morning.

Chhaiya : Where is Chandni?

Saanvi : She is in the room.

Chandni : She is ready?

    Saanvi with anger :

Saanvi : I don't know.

    She left from there. Chhaiya got confuse. She goes to Chandni's room, Chandni is still sleeping.

Chhaiya : Chandni. …..! You are still sleeping? Wake up, you don't want to go college?

Chandni : Chhaiya, please get out from here, I am not going anywhere.

Chhaiya : Why? Are you unwell?

Chandni : yes, now go.

Chhaiya checks her temperature. Chandni angrily:

Chandni : What are you doing?

Chhaiya : You are perfectly fine.

Chandni controlling herself.

Chandni : Chhaiya, please, I don't want to go college, you just go from here.

Chhaiya : But why? what is the matter, why don't you want to go college?

The Dark Moon

Chandni : Nothing, I just don't want to go college, why don't you understand?

Chhaiya : There is some problem? share with me, I am your best friend.

Chandni got furious :

Chandni : You are not my best friend, You and I have never been friends, because of you, our friendship got the name Black and White, People weren't looking at me before you, because of you, people started laughing at me, whoever sees us, they calls us black and white, I have seen you that you don't care about it, but I care.

Chhaiya got confuse :

Chhaiya : Has anyone said anything to you?

Chandni : Ever since we became friends, people have been saying.

Chhaiya : Chandni, relax, why don't you ignore all of this and them?

Chandni : I have only one way, to correct myself.

Chhaiya : please tell me, and I will help you.

Chandni : you have to leave from my life, I don't want this name anymore.

    Chhaiya came up to her bedroom, she has tears in her eyes. She close her eyes, and thinking about Chandni's words and started crying.

Kahkashan Zaid

        Chandni start ignoring Chhaiya. Chhaiya used to try to talk to her, but Chandni do not want to talk to her.

        Chhaiya was upset, she was not eating properly, her parents saw, Chhaiya was crying in her room, her parents came to talk to her :

Seema   : Chhaiya?

        She hides her tears.

Chhaiya : Yes mom.

        Both looked at her, her face is red, and her eyes is red :

Vinod   : Are you crying?

Seema   : look at me!

        Chhaiya's eyes were full of tears, she hug her mom and started crying.

        Chhaiya told everything to both of them, what Chandni has told her, and how she is ignoring her.

        Chhaiya calmly says :

Chhaiya : do you guys remember? When I was young, I used to feel insecure about myself, I remember, one day I was very worried about this genetic problem, and grandma told me.

        7 years old Chhaiya. She was sitting alone in her garden, with so many children playing with each other. her grandma she is

The Dark Moon

also an Albinism woman, she came up to her:

Grandma: Chhaiya? What happen my child? Are you upset?

Chhaiya start crying. Grandma got tense :

Grandma: What happen my child, anyone said anything to you? Why are you crying?

Chhaiya says while crying :

Chhaiya : Everyone calls me white ghost, and no one kid play with me, they think, I am real white ghost.

Grandma start laughing, Chhaiya start crying :

Chhaiya : You also laughing at me.

Grandma stop laughing :

Grandma: I am not laughing at you my child, don't think that I am laughing at you.

Chhaiya : Then why are you laughing at me?

Grandma: First, stop wasting your precious tears, your tears are just not a tears, is diamond for us.

She cleans her face :

Grandma: That's my girl, let's go.

Chhaiya : Where is grandma?

Grandma: To answer all you questions.

Chhaiya : but where grandma?

Grandma: I will tell you everything, first help me to stand me up.

She helps her.

Kahkashan Zaid

Chhaiya : Grandma, you are so heavy!

Grandma: Chhaiya.......!

Chhaiya : Sorry.

    Both do walking :

Chhaiya : But Grandma, where are we going?

Grandma: Now if you ask me one more time, we'll go home.

Chhaiya : Ok Grandma .

Grandma: Good girl.

    They came up under the Mango tree.

Chhaiya : Grandma! Why are we here?

Grandma: look at the tree.

Chhaiya : ooh, this is a mango tree.

Grandma: you tell me one thing.

Chhaiya : Yes?

Grandma: This tree has two types of mangos, one is tasty, and delicious and the second is vain mango, what would you choose?

Chhaiya : Grandma, of course, I will choose tasty and delicious mango.

Grandma: and what will you do with vain mango?

Chhaiya : I will throw into the dustbin, what will I do with it?

Grandma: And what about tree?

Chhaiya : means?

Grandma: I mean, you cut the tree or not?

The Dark Moon

Chhaiya : why I will cut the tree, it giving me tasty and delicious mangos.

Grandma: this is what I am trying to teach you.

Chhaiya : What!

Grandma: you have lack of intelligence.

Chhaiya : Grandma…..!

Grandma: okay, this tree gives us two types of mangos, one is testy and the second is vain, you choose tastily and throw vain mangos, and you also not cut the tree, because the tree gives you tasty mangos, similarly, human also have two types of qualities, good qualities and bad qualities, the wise human accept their bad qualities, and they focus and improve their good qualities, you have a genetic problem, but you have something, which nobody has, and you need to find it out, and moreover, you need to build you Positive attitude, whoever says you and laugh at you, just smile, if you will not smile, they will more laugh at you, and it will happen when you accept yourself the way you are, understood?

Chhaiya : Trying to understand.

Grandma: Chhaiya….!

Chhaiya : Grandma, you said a lot of things , it will take time to understand, but I do understand one thing very clearly , if someone laughs at you, you have to smile.

Present time :

Chhaiya : Where Grandma would take me, and whatever she told me, I still remember, After Grandma left, I would be alone for a while, not only Grandma would leave me that day, I would leave my friend, whenever people made fun of me, I remembered Grandma's words and I smiled.

Vinod : When mom left us, you changed a lot, you started misbehaving in your school, principal rusticate you, but since you were with Chandni, you would be like before.

Chhaiya : Maybe, I am being as rude as before, I do not like anything, I get angry at everything, but I don't want to Express my feelings, what should I do, mom?

Seema : First, you have to relax, you don't need to change yourself, she need to change herself, and you have to help her.

Vinod : Your mom is right.

Chhaiya : But how?

Vinod : Like your Grandma did.

Chhaiya understood her parents words:

Chhaiya : Understood.

In college :

Lunch time. The two are having their lunch at different table.

Aarav came up to Chandni :

Aarav : Hey? May I sit over here?

Chandni : Nope.

The Dark Moon

Aarav sat :

Aarav : Thank you.

Chandni angrily :

Chandni : But I said no.

Aarav : Relax, why are you shouting! everyone is watching us.

Chandni slowly :

Chandni : But I told you not to sit here, and you sat here!

Aarav : Actually, I need your help.

Chandni : But I can not help you.

Aarav : Listen first.

Chandni : I think I should go from here.

Aarav : Hey stop, please, at least listen to me.

She returned to her seat. Chhaiya was watching both of them.

Chandni : What's wrong with you?

Aarav : why are you so rude?

She started staring at him.

Aarav : Sorry, actually, you are a bright student, could you please help me in my study, because the semester is about to come.

Chandni : How did you know, that I am a bright student?

Aarav : Your friend White told me.

Chandni started staring at Chhaiya.

Chandni : First of all, her name is, Chhaiya.

Aarav   : sorry, I did not know, and your name?
Chandni : you don't know my name?
Aarav   : That's why I am asking you, actually, you guys are famous as black and white, that's why most people don't know your name, and I am one of them.

    Chandni says nothing.

Aarav   : your name?
Chandni : hmmm?
Aarav   : name, your name?
Chandni : Chandni.
Aarav   : ooh, nice name, my name is Aarav, so, would you help me?
Chandni : okay.
Aarav   : Thank you so much.

    Chandni having her lunch.

Aarav   : so, when do we start?
Chandni : have lunch first?
Aarav   : sure.

    Aarav gave a tumb to Chhaiya.

    After college :

    Aarav stopping Chhaiya :

Aarav   : hey stop, Chhaiya.

    Both are walking.

Chhaiya : what happened?
Aarav   : Why are you helping me?

The Dark Moon

Chhaiya : who told you, that I am helping you, I am helping my friend, Chandni.

Aarav : How?

Chhaiya : She is brilliant in her studies. Her dream is to become a Journalist, whoever I am today because of her, she helped me a lot in my study, and she will also help you.

Aarav : I have a question.

Chhaiya : Ask.

Aarav : Whatever Benefits will be mine, what will be the benefit for her?

Chhaiya : That girl is only paying attention to her shortcomings, she does not see the talent inside her, I want you to tell her how talented she is.

Aarav : Why do not you do that? you can also do that.

Chhaiya : Actually, she upset with me.

Aarav : Why?

Chhaiya : Um..., she thinks that the name black and white is come from me.

Aarav : What!

Chhaiya : do you help me?

Aarav : Hmmm, of course.

    Both smiling.

    Both are studying in the library.

Aarav : Chandni?

Chandni : hmmm?

Kahkashan Zaid

Aarav : Please help me, I do not understand.

          Chandni Angrily :

Chandni : I have taught you 6th times, why do not you understand?

          The whole library is watching both of them. Aarav get upset.

          He is sit alone in the campus, Chhaiya came up to him :

Chhaiya : Hey?

          She saw that, he is upset :

Chhaiya : What happen? You looking upset.

Aarav : Chandni scolded me.

Chhaiya : ooh, it's ok.

Aarav : why it's ok? Your friend is so……

Chhaiya : what……!

Aarav : so dangerous.

Chhaiya : see, she is not fine inside, try to understand.

Aarav : so what, she will take out her anger on me? so what happen, if I questioned the same question in 7th time?

Chhaiya : What…..! 7th times! You are weaker in studies than me.

Aarav : she ever scolded you like this?

Chhaiya : I'm not as dumb as you.

Aarav : Chhaiya……!

Chhaiya : what Chhaiya!

          She started Laughing at him.

The Dark Moon

Chhaiya : I'm not as dumb as you.

After coming from the Chandni, he started spending time with Chhaiya, he started liking her, and slowly, slowly she also started liking him. they started spending more time with each other.

One day, Chandni sees the two from afar, she started smiling.

Chandni asks Aarav in library :

Chandni : We have finished the syllabus, After a week, exam will about to start, you memorized everything?

Aarav get nervous :

Aarav : Aa……..a!!!

Chandni angrily :

Chandni : Aarav…….!

Aarav : I memorized everything, but the problem is, what if I forgot in the exam hall?

Chandni : If you memorized everything, then don't worry, when you see the question, you will quickly remember the answer, if you have any questions, please clear now, otherwise, I will not help you anymore.

Aarav : I have a question.

Chandni : Ask!

Aarav : why are you always in bad mood?

Chandni sees Aarav angrily :

Aarav : you told me to ask a question.

~ 25 ~

Chandni : Not personal, ask any questions about studies.

Aarav : But seriously, why are you always in bad mood, you have brilliant mind, why are you not happy with yourself?

Chandni : Can't you see? that nobody is with me? how can I happy?

Aarav : who was with you, you remove from your life, Yet, you are not happy alone, you are not with anyone, you do not want to be happy, that's why you are never happy.

Chandni : it is easy to say anything, you were also come up to me, because, you want good marks in studies.

Aarav : yes right, but we are also friends, isn't ?

Chandni : we are not friends, we just classmates.

She was just going. Aarav angrily :

Aarav : if you have a massive problem with your color, then why don't you use whitening injection.

Chandni got shock, Aarav realized that, he said wrong and the whole library students watching them.

Aarav : Chandni......, I am sorry.

Chandni had tears in her eyes, she left from there. Aarav says to himself :

Aarav : ooh shit, what I did!

The Dark Moon

          In a corridor, Chhaiya sees Chandni with tears in her eyes, Aarav come out from library, Chhaiya asks Aarav :

Chhaiya : What happened? Why she has tears in her eyes? Has anyone said anything to her?

Aarav : Shall we go to the garden?

Chhaiya : No, say first, what happened with her, why she has tears in her eyes?

Aarav : first let's go to the garden.

          Both sit in the garden, Aarav told everything to Chhaiya, she is staring him, and says angrily :

Chhaiya : I you mad or what? Why did you say that to her?

Aarav : I know, I did wrong, but trust me, it was unintentional, nothing i did intentionally, please trust me!

          Chhaiya says upsetly :

Chhaiya : How bad she must have felt!

Aarav : you don't worry, after a while, I will meet her, and will say sorry to her.

          Chhaiya is angry at him. Chandni is sit alone, she reciting book, Aarav came up to her :

Aarav : hey!

          She did not answer :

Aarav : Chandni sorry, I shouldn't have said that.

Chandni : It's ok.

Aarav : you don't upset with me?
Chandni : Nope.
Aarav : means, we are friends?
Chandni : friends.
Aarav : So now befriend her, who is truly your friend.
Chandni : you want to be a friend or not?
Aarav : friends.

    Both do a handshake.

After the first exam :

    Chandni is waiting for Aarav. He came out from the exam hall :

Chandni : how was your exam?

    He pretends that he gave an excellent exam. Aarav enthusiastically :

Aarav : excellent, how was your?
Chandni : mine was excellent, your marks will tell your performance.

    He left from there, and says himself :

Aarav : my performance was terrible, what she will do with me?

    Chandni said herself :

Chandni : his enthusiastic telling his nervousness.

    Chhaiya Asks Aarav in the garden :

Chhaiya : how was your exam?
Aarav : terrible.
Chhaiya : what! But you prepared well, right?

The Dark Moon

Aarav : yes, whatever I understood over there, I wrote it and came out.

Chhaiya : will you pass or?

Aarav :

Chhaiya : I hope so from you.

everyday Chandni asks Aarav, how his exam going, and he always pretends that he gives an excellent exam.

Exam over :

few days lapse, the results list is put on the list board. Aarav checking his Marks:

Aarav : please side, please, oh nooooo!

He get shocked, He came out from the crowd. Chandni sitting over there, she asks him :

Chandni : what happened?

Aarav happily hug Chandni :

Aarav : thank you, I got 4th position.

Chandni happily says :

Chandni : wowwwww, congratulations.

Aarav : thank you.

Chandni : and, what about Chhaiya?

Aarav : I don't know.

Meanwhile, Chhaiya came up to them, she happily hugs Chandni :

Chhaiya : I got 3rd position and you got 1st position.

Kahkashan Zaid

        Chandni gets shocked, she realized, that she hugs Chhaiya. She about to go from there :

Chhaiya : Chandni! Listen to me.

        But she left from there. Chhaiya got upset.

Aarav   : It's ok Chhaiya, don't mind, let's go.

Chhaiya : you tell me one thing!

Aarav   : what?

Chhaiya : you always said that your exam was damn bad.

Aarav   : But I also said that, what I understood over there, I wrote, and came out.

Chhaiya : okay, let's go.

Both left from there.

3 years later :

        Their convocation day. Everybody Is happy, and clicking pictures. Chandni sit alone, like always. Chhaiya sees her, and goes to her:

Chhaiya : Chandni?

Chandni : hmmmm?

Chhaiya : why are you sit over here? let's click pictures together.

Chandni : why don't you understand, I don't want to be with you.

Meanwhile while Aarav came up to them.

Aarav   : what's up girls? Let's click pictures together?

Chandni : Nope.

Aarav   : okay, thank you.

The Dark Moon

    Aarav took Chandni and Chhaiya stand with him :

Chandni : what you doing, I said no.

Aarav : I know, cameraman, click our pictures.

    Chhaiya is so happy. They clicking pictures with smile. When Aarav Saw the pictures, he says to Chandni :

Chandni : wow...., bro your smile is damn cute, why don't you smile all the time? I saw your smile for the first time.

    Chandni give a massive smile. Chhaiya is so happy to her. They having fun their convocation day.

    Few days later.

    While having dinner, Chhaiya's parents to Chhaiya and Chandni's parents to Chandni:

Viraj   : Chandni? What is your next plan?

Chandni : I applied for some TV channels for interview.

Seema : do you think, they will approach you?

Chhaiya : why not mom?

Saanvi : why are you feeling!

Chandni : don't start again.

Viraj   : why, you need to understand, your are not TV face.

Chhaiya : why are you guys talking about this?

Vinod : TV wants a beautiful face, and you.

Chandni : Confidence has never been born in me, you know why? only because of you guys.

Chandni left from there. Chhaiya very smoothly and calmly said to her parents :

Chhaiya : Dad relax, If they approach me is good, if they don't is probably very good, I just want to try my best, I don't want to get regrets, that I didn't try.

Seema : I am proud of you my child.

Chhaiya : I am also proud of myself, I don't know why, But I am so cool, right, Dad?

Vinod : right.

They enjoying their dinner.

Chhaiya and Chandni getting ready for their interview :

Chhaiya leaves her room happily and confidently, Seema and Vinod are waiting for her with yogurt sugar. She came up to them, seema Feeds her one tablespoon of yogurt sugar.

Seema : Best of luck for your interview.

Chhaiya : thank you mom.

Vinod : give your best.

Chhaiya : yes dad, bye mom, bye dad.

Both together : bye dear.

Chhaiya left from her house.

Chandni came up from her room, happily and very confidently, she came up to Viraj and Saanvi.

Chandni : mom, I am going to give my first interview.

The Dark Moon

Saanvi : you are not for this job, but if you trying, best of luck.

Chandni Angrily :

Chandni : I wish I didn't tell you that.

    She left from her house. Divya sees Chandni, she asks her :

Divya : hey Chandni!

    Chandni gets tensed seeing her:

Divya : where are you going?

Chandni : um… …, today is my interview.

Divya : ooh, I don't think you will get this job, but All the best.

    Chandni got Angry, but reply with smile:

Chandni : thank you Aunty.

Divya : Bye.

Chandni : bye.

    She left from there place. One is a happy and one is a sad.

    Both are coming on the same TV News channel. Both are waiting for their turn.

Chhaiya asks receptionist :

Chhaiya : When will our turn come?

Receptionist: You wait, when your turn comes, you will be told.

Chhaiya : okay.

    Chhaiya back to her seat. Everyone gets interviews. The receptionist comes to both of them :

Receptionist: Chhaiya and Chandni, You both leave from here, the interview time is over.

Chandni : but we did not give an interview!

Receptionist : We have sucked our candidate, so the interview is over.

Chhaiya angrily :

Chhaiya : What are you saying, we came here to give an interview, and without takeing our interview, you sucked your candidate!

Receptionist : I tell you clearly, We cannot give this job to both of you.

Chhaiya : why?

Receptionist : ma'am......!

Chandni : it's ok, let's go Chhaiya.

Chandni takes Chhaiya's hand and takes her from there. Chandni Chhaiya comes outside. Chhaiya angrily:

Chhaiya : Why did you bring me here from there, I would have broken their face.

Chandni : That's why I have brought you here from there.

Chhaiya : There was no problem if They rejected us after taking interview, but these people did wrong, you don't get upset, we try to find another place.

Chandni got upset and left from there.

Meanwhile Chhaiya's phone ringing:

Chhaiya : hello Aarav.

The Dark Moon

Aarav : I got the job.

Chhaiya : ooh, congratulations.

Aarav : thank you, and what about you?

Chhaiya : they didn't take our interview.

Aarav : Huh, our?

Chhaiya : Chandni and mine.

Aarav : but why they didn't take your interview?

Chhaiya comes home, seema asks Chhaiya:

Seema : Chhaiya!

Chhaiya : hey mom.

Seema : how was your interview?

Chhaiya : terrible.

Seema : it's ok dear, don't lose your confidence, better luck next time.

Chhaiya : thank you, mom, your words give me the courage and build my confidence, love you Mom.

Seema : love you dear, go and rest.

She goes to her room.

Chandni coming up towards her house. She saw Divya, and she secretly going from there, Divya saw her, Divya asks Chandni:

Divya : hey Chandni! How was your interview?

Chandni : you sit over here, so that, you can ask me this question?

Divya : of course, Now tell me, how was your interview? I think, you didn't get the job! Right?

~ 35 ~

Chandni : Carved question, carved answer, right.

Divya : I knew it.

> Chandni angrily left from there, she entered at her home. Saanvi asks Chandni :

Saanvi : Chandni!

Chandni : hey mom.

Saanvi : how was your interview?

Chandni's face is very upset.

Saanvi : your face telling, that your interview was not good at all, I told you, that you are not fit for this job.

> Chandni has tears in her eyes, and says very sadly:

Chandni : please mom, if you not saying good words, then you don't need to say negative words also, your words break my confidant, break my hopes, break my heart, and most important thing, it impact my peace of mind.

Saanvi : I am telling the truth, why don't you understand?

Chandni : talking to you, is just a waste of time, don't disturb me.

Chandni goes to her room :

Saanvi : Chandni listen to me?

> She locked herself in the room, and crying very badly, without a sound.
>
> Both used to go to the same TV news channels to give interviews, at many places,

The Dark Moon

two were interviewed, but they were not selected, And in many places the interview of both was not taken.

2 years later. Aarav and Chhaiya at the cafe:

Aarav : Chhaiya, please accept my point.

Chhaiya : But Aarav……

Aarav : what Aarav, you did try for 2 years, it didn't happen, it's ok, and if you want to try further, then you can do that even after marriage, pleaseeeeee!

Chhaiya : okay, I will talk to my parents, by the way coffee is so tasty.

Aarav : true.

Chhaiya came up to her parents room, she silently sat over there, she didn't say anything.

Seema : what happened? do you want to say something?

Chhaiya got nervous :

Chhaiya : yes mom.

Vinod : what dear?

Chhaiya : aaaa actually, I love someone.

Both together : Oooooo.

Vinod : whom?

Chhaiya : he was my classmate in college.

Seema : what his name?

Chhaiya : Aarav.

Vinod : So, when are you meeting us?

Kahkashan Zaid

Chhaiya happily :

Chhaiya : Tomorrow?

Both together:ok.

She hugs both of them :

Chhaiya : thank you Mom and dad.

Couple of days later :

> The wedding day.
>
> Both are so happy, Chandni came up to their wedding, she hugs both of them andcongratulates them. The dance happening over there, everyone is happy.

Chhaiya says to Chandni :

Chhaiya : thank you!

Chandni : for what?

Chhaiya : to come back into my life.

Chandni : sorry!

Chhaiya : for what?

Chandni : To hurt you.

Chhaiya : it's ok, why are you always anxious about your skin color?

Chandni : today is you big day, can we discuss this things another day?

Chhaiya : love you.

Aarav came up to them :

Aarav : love you too.

Chhaiya : I didn't say to you.

Aarav : then?

The Dark Moon

Chandni : she said to me.

Aarav : Huh, If I had known that both of you would be together on the wedding day, we would have got married earlier.

Chandni : shut up, I am happy for both of you.

Chandni says to Aarav :

Chandni : Always be with her, and Chhaiya, always be with him, by the way, where you guys going for honeymoon?

Chhaiya : we didn't decide.

Aarav : Chandni, You also get married, then we will go together on honeymoon.

Chhaiya : what....!

Aarav : I mean, I with you, and she with her spouse.

Chhaiya : nice idea.

Chandni : we discussing all this things on yours stage, please attend your guests, someone coming towards us.

Guest : Congratulations.

Both together : thank you.

Chandni got upset going from there.

A few days later, at the dinning table, Viraj says to Chandni :

Viraj : Chandni!

Chandni : yes Dad?

Viraj : I think you should get married, now your friend has also got married.

Saanvi : After a few days, they will come to see you.

Kahkashan Zaid

Chhaiya : Mom....!

Saanvi : Those people were coming tomorrow, we said they come after a few days, as long as your color will be a little right.

Chhaiya : The color which was not correct in 24 years, will be correct in a few days, because of you guys, I could never move forward, remember this much.

Viraj : Why are you always rude with us?

Chhaiya : ask yourself Dad, you will get your answer.

She left from there :

Saanvi : Finish your dinner at least!

Viraj : don't know what will happen with her.

Saanvi : don't worry, please have your dinner.

Viraj : teach her, how to behave with your parents.

Next morning :

Chandni open her eyes, and saanvi stands in front of her, she was afraid :

Chandni : Mom....! What are you doing?

Saanvi : get up, and apply this turmeric paste.

Chandni : why!

Saanvi : it will glow your face.

Chandni very sadly :

Chandni : mom please...., don't do this to me.

Saanvi very politely :

Saanvi : my dear, please listen to me, do it for me.

Chandni : you never talk to me like this before!

~ 40 ~

The Dark Moon

Saanvi : Means, you will do?

Chandni : Said with so much love, who can disobey?

> Saanvi applied turmeric paste on her face.
>
> In the morning and evening, Saanvi would put something on her face, she gives water to drink, There was a restriction on her going out, so that she would not turn black.
>
> At Evening Chhaiya call Chandni.

Chandni : hello Chhaiya!

Chhaiya : where are you?

Chandni : I am at home, why are you asking?

Chhaiya : nothing, just asking, let's meet up.

Chandni : aaaaaa, but…..

Chhaiya : It's been so many days, since we haven't met.

Chandni : I know, ok fine, let's meet up.

> She is getting ready to go out. Chandni is hiding and going out. Saanvi saw her:

Saanvi : Stop Chandni!

Chandni : shit…..! Yes mom?

Saanvi : where are you going?

Chandni : Mom please, It's been 4 days, I haven't gone out of the house, let me go outside.

Saanvi : Why do you want to darken yourself in the sun?

Chandni : How much more will I darken the black?

Saanvi : I said go to your room.

Chandni : ok fine.

Chandni angrily goes to her room.

She calls Chhaiya :

Chhaiya : hello? did you leave the house?

Chandni : sorry, I am not coming.

Chhaiya : why?

Chandni : Actually.......

She tells everything to her :

Chhaiya : Huh, it's ok.

Chandni : ok bye.

Chhaiya : bye.

Phone cut:

Chhaiya : poor Chandni.

At night, Chhaiya's room, she is thinking about Chandni, Aarav asks her :

Aarav : what happened? What are you thinking about?

Chhaiya : I am thinking about Chandni.

Aarav : why? What happened to her?

Chhaiya : As my family supported me in everything, I wish Chandni's family also supported her.

Aarav : something is happened?

Chhaiya : Saanvi Aunty and Viraj's Uncle have always told Chandni a lot about her complexion, made her realize how bad her complexion is.

Aarav : hmmm, Don't know how many parents out there, who do all this things.

The Dark Moon

Chhaiya : countless people.

Aarav : don't think so much, about what we can do!

Chhaiya : wish could we do something.

Aarav : it's ok.

Chhaiya is worried about Chandni. She says in her mind:

Chhaiya : I hope, In her life, someone should come like that, like her the way she is.

A few days later :

Saanvi says to Chandni in her room :

Chandni : mommmm!

Saanvi : shut up, Tomorrow those people are coming to meet you, apply this turmeric paste, and relax, tomorrow you should look fresh.

Chandni : Mom….., Why are you torturing me?

Saanvi : Think whatever you want to think, and anyway, this torture happens to every girl who has the same complexion as you have, so don't consider yourself alone.

Chandni : Don't know about everyone, but the girl who has parents like you, with them this is the biggest torture.

Saanvi : Chandni…..!

Chandni : give this turmeric paste, You meet me tomorrow only.

Saanvi : I will ask you the day you have a black daughter.

Kahkashan Zaid

>Saanvi left from there. Chandni looks at herself in the mirror, applying turmeric paste and saying angrily :

Chandni : Did you think that I was named Chandni? As is the face, so is the fate, ugly.

Next day :

Neel's family comes to see Chandni, Neel's dad, Sumesh :

Sumesh : oh bro, You guys have made a lot of arrangements.

Viraj : oh bro, where is that much? Only a little has been done.

>Neel's mom Aachal :

Aachal : how are you guys?

Seema : We are all very good, did you guys have any problem in finding a home?

Aachal : Nope, There was no problem.

Viraj : This is a very good thing, you guys take something.

Both of them : yes.

Viraj : Neel dear, please eat something.

Neel : yes uncle.

>They are talking to each other.

>Chandni is in her room and taking to Chhaiya on a video call, Chandni is in tension :

Chhaiya : Chandni relax, why are you getting tense? Please stay calm.

The Dark Moon

Chandni : what are you saying, The boys have come outside to see me and you are saying stay calm! How!

Chhaiya : First of all, sit comfortably in one place.

Chandni : Chhaiya……

Chhaiya : please listen to me, sit calmly.

    Chandni sits calmly.

Chhaiya : take a deep breath.

    Chandni takes deep breath.

Chhaiya : Chandni be confident, okay!

Chandni shaking her head : (ok).

Chhaiya : good girl.

Chandni : I am looking great.

Chhaiya : are you ready?

Chandni : of course, now tell me, how it is?

Chhaiya : why are you looking so simple?

Chandni : why? I am not looking good.

Chhaiya : everything is perfect, but please, wear a jhumka, it will look great on a black outfit.

Chandni : Which? This or that?

Chhaiya : this.

Chandni wear a jhumka :

Chandni : see, it is good?

Chhaiya : perfect my love.

Chandni : thank you.

~ 45 ~

Kahkashan Zaid

Chhaiya : okay, I am going to cut the call, and be confident, talk confidently, sit confidently, over all you have to be confident, okay?

Chandni : okay.

Chhaiya : All the best, bye.

Chandni : bye.

Video call cut :

Chhaiya : God please, give her confident.

    Aachal says Seema :

Aachal : Seema sister, call your daughter, she is ready?

Seema : yeah, I bring her.

    Seema goes to Chandni's room, when she sees her in a black outfit :

Seema : Chandni.....!

Chandni : have you come to pick me up?

Seem : yes, but why are you wear a black outfit?

Chandni : why? I am not looking great ?

Seema : it's ok, You come to the living room with a tray of tea from the kitchen, okay?

Chandni : okay Mom.

Seema : I go, you come.

Chandni : okay Mom.

Seema left from there. Chandni looks at herself in the mirror, and took deep breath :

Chandni : be confident.

Seema came up in living room :

The Dark Moon

Viraj : where is Chandni?

Chandni : she is coming.

Aachal : Seema sister, where is your daughter Chandni?

Seema : she is coming.

Sumesh : I hope she is looking like her name, Chandni, what a beautiful name you choose for your daughter.

Seema and Viraj got nervous :

Seema : yes……

    Chandni walks into the living room smiling with a tray of tea, she greets everyone. Three of them with smile :

Three of them : Namaste.

Aachal : who is she? She is your maid?

    Chandni look at her parents :

Viraj : Nope.

Sumesh : whoever she is, please call your daughter Chandni, since when have we been waiting for her?

Chandni has tears in her eyes :

Seema : she is Chandni.

    Three of them stand up, and are shocked :

Aachal : what…..! She is Chandni? Where from?

    Chandni lost her confidence, and start shivering.

Sumesh : are you kidding with us, why did you choose this name for her?

Kahkashan Zaid

Aachal	: How did you guys think that we will make this black stain the moon of our house?
Seema	: listen.
Aachal	: you listen, Keep the stain of this moon with you, let's go Sumesh.
Sumesh	: let's go.

Three of them going from there :

Viraj	: Sumesh bro, my daughter is good from nature.
Aachal	: What will we do with nature, when there is no beauty, then we also have to show our face to everyone in our family, And anyway there is no connection between my son and your daughter Chandni Moon, and when the moon is like this, not at all.
Sumesh	: Leave our way.

Viraj and Seema moved away from the front. The three of them left from there. Divya saw:

Divya	: It seems, they have rejected her, I told Seema, but she did not listen to me, This is not my concern.

Divya goes inside.

Saanvi angrily says to Chandni :

Saanvi	: Get away from my eyes, who told you to wear a black dress on this black color! Who told you? Go, Go to your room.

Viraj politely :

Chandni	: Chandni dear, please go to your room.

The Dark Moon

        Chandni had tears in her eyes and goes to her room. Viraj says to Saanvi :

Viraj : What is her fault in this, you should not have talked to her like this.

Saanvi : Our luck, that we have got a black daughter.

Viraj : what we can do?

Chhaiya is tension, and walking into her room, and says to herself :

Chhaiya : Don't know what will be happening to Chandni, call her. No, now she must be sitting with everyone, if those people leave, then she will call me.

        Chandni locks herself in the bathroom and is sitting by the door. she remembers the things of the words of Aachal, her hands start shivering. Slowly all the taunts of her life start to be heard from her mind, Divya's, Ananya's, Aarav's, her parents and she slowly starts screaming :

Chandni : Nope, Noooooo, Nooooooo, everyone shut up, everyone shut up, no one says anything to me, what should I do if I am like this?

        Saanvi and Viraj are heard screaming and they quickly go to her room :

Viraj : Chandni dear, are you okay, please open the door.

        Chandni is screaming :

Chandni : aaaaaaaaa, aaaaaaaaaa, I am like this, what is my fault for that?

~ *49* ~

Saanvi : Chandni! Chandni... ....!, open the door dear, please......

Chandni angrily starts scrubbing herself with the help of a scrubber, on her face, on her hand, and all over her body. Bleeding starts from her body, she is crying and screaming.

Saanvi is crying :

Saanvi : Viraj do something, break down the door.

Viraj : okay.

Saanvi : Chandni please ......, Chandni open the door.

Viraj starts breaking the door. After trying hard, Viraj breaks down the door. Both go to Chandni :

Saanvi : Chandni....., Chandni dear...., are you okay? Blood!

Chandni : mom, what is my fault, if I am black, I have not created myself, what should I do if I am like this? Aaaaaaaaa.

Chandni starts to faint because of screaming :

Chandni : mom! What is my mistake? What is my mistake? What... ....is... my..... mistake?

She faints.

Viraj : Chandni! Chandni! Wake up dear!

Saanvi : Viraj....... !

Viraj : We will have to take her to the hospital.

Both take her to the hospital, blood is coming out from her body.

It is evening, Aarav comes from the office, and sees Chhaiyatension :

Aarav : what do you think?

Chhaiya : I am waiting.

Aarav : For what?

Chhaiya : Chandni's call.

Aarav : Why?

She tells everything to him :

Aarav : ooh, but why don't you call her?

Chhaiya : But she must not have called for some reason.

Aarav : You think a lot.

Chhaiya : Okay fine, I call her.

Chhaiya calls Chandni, Chandni's phone is in her room.

Chhaiya : She is not pick up my call!

Aarav : She must be engrossed somewhere, try it one more time.

Chhaiya trying again.

Chhaiya : she is not picking up.

Aarav : but why.

Meanwhile Saanvi call her :

Chhaiya : Auntie's phone!

She pick her call :

Chhaiya : hello Aunty.

Saanvi tells him everything, she gets shocked hearing it, and tears well in her eyes.

Aarav : What happened Chhaiya?

Chhaiya : Chandni.......!

The doctor came up to Saanvi and Viraj:

Viraj : Doctor, how is Chandni?

Doctor : She is still unconscious, it's okay, she fainted, otherwise her nerves could have burst due to tension, Chandni has scrubbed her entire body vigorously, but she is quiet rightnow waiting for her to come to her senses.

Doctor left from there, meanwhile Chhaiya and Aarav came up there :

Chhaiya : Aunty, how she is?

Saanvi hugs Chhaiya while crying.

Chhaiya : Please don't cry.

Aarav : What did the doctor say? How is her condition now?

Viraj : she is unconscious, but she is fine, the doctor has said, let's wait for her to come to her senses.

Chhaiya : everything will be alright.

Saanvi : Everything has happened because of us, I wish we never made her realize that her complexion is bad.

Chhaiya : it is okay, now you guys realized, she will soon realize too, that her color is not bad, people's perceptions is bad.

The Dark Moon

            It's night. Chandni is not conscious:

Saanvi : Chhaiya dear! You and Aarav go home, we Stay.

Aarav : it's ok Aunty, I know, Chhaiya will not leave Chandni.

Viraj : but dear…..!

Chhaiya : please Uncle, I will not go, in fact, you guys go home, otherwise your health will get worse.

Saanvi : not at all.

Chhaiya : Aunty pleaseeeeeee!

Viraj : but…..

Both together : please Uncle!

Both together : Okay.

Aarav : I will drop you both at home.

            Next day.

            Chandni is sitting quietly, the doctor is checking her.

Doctor : Chandni! how are you feeling now?

Chandni doesn't say anything :

Doctor : I think she is in shock.

Saanvi : Doctor, she will be fine?

Doctor : Now medicine is not needed for her, a good palace is needed, all of you try to not give her stress, okay?

All together : okay.

Viraj : When can we discharge her?

Kahkashan Zaid

Doctor : Today, complete your discharge formalities.

Viraj : okay

> The doctor left there. Viraj also follows him. Saanvi holds Chandni's hand, and Chandni releases her hand from her.
>
> Chhaiya gestures to Aarav to take Saanvi out.

Aarav : Aunty, let's go outside.

Saanvi : but.

Aarav : Just going outside.

> Both left from room. Chandni starts hearing everything again, Chhaiya is holding her hand, Chandni stops hearing. Chhaiya kisses her hand, and looks at her with a smile.

Chhaiya : are you okay?

She doesn't say anything :

Chhaiya : Chandni? Chandni look at me, I don't know what you are feeling, but life has given you a lot of chances, now it's your turn, The doctor has said that you need a good place, we will go far away from this place for a few days, But when you come, we all need a new Chandni, shining just like the moon, You always say why are you named Chandni? You have to find the answer for yourself, and this answer will not be found by looking at your inner shortcomings, Look at the

The Dark Moon

good inside you, what are you, and why are you.

A few days later, Chandni Chhaiya and Aarav are about to leave for Budapest:

Saanvi : Chhaiya, please take care of her.

Chhaiya : Don't worry Aunty, bye.

Everyone is leaving in the car, Divya to Chandni:

Divya : Darky! Where are you going?

Chhaiya is going towards Divya in anger, Aarav stops her :

Aarav : let it be, we getting late, let's go.

All three sit in the car and leave for the airport.

Divya : don't know, where they are going, this is not my concern.

Interval :

The three of them airports reach :

Chhaiya : Aarav, you took everything?

Aarav : yes.

All three in the plane :

Chandni and Chhaiya are seated together, and Aarav is on a different seat. Chandni to Chhaiya :

Chandni : You are here because of me, I go to Aarav's seat, and send him here.

Chhaiya : no need to do this.

Chandni : need to do this.

Chandni goes to Aarav :

Aarav : what happened Chandni?

Chandni : You go to my seat, I sit on your seat.

Aarav : umm... , okay, but you, alone!

Chandni : it's ok, you go.

Aarav goes to Chhaiya, and Chandni sits on Aarav's seat.

Aarav to Chhaiya :

Aarav : what happened?

Chhaiya : nothing, we are both far away from each other, and she felt guilty.

Aarav : I didn't even talk to her much, I have a window seat, she sat there, so she likes it.

Chhaiya : good.

Chandni is looking outside while sitting on the window seat. At the same time, Reyansh sits on the seat next to Chandni, Chandni is silently looking outside. Reyansh keeps looking at her.

Everyone is sleeping in the plane at night, Chandni started hearing everyone's words again in her dream, She grabs Reyansh's hand tightly, Reyansh breaks his sleep, because of Chandni's nails, bleeding start from his hand, He lives in pain, Reyansh shakes her vigorously, Chandni wakes up in fear. She let's go of his hand :

Chandni : ooh, so sorry.

The Dark Moon

And goes to the washroom. Reyansh sees blood in his hand. Chandni comes out of the washroom, Reyansh stands outside the washroom, he hides his hand. Chandni goes to her seat and sits down. Chhaiya looks at her, and asks her :

Chhaiya : are you okay? where did you go?

Chandni : I'm fine, I went to the washroom.

Chhaiya : Where did the passenger who next to you ?

Reyansh knocks Chhaiya:

Chhaiya : ooh, sorry.

Chandni : You go to sleep, I'm fine.

Chhaiya : okay fine.

Chhaiya goes to her seat.

Aarav : where did you go?

Chhaiya : Went to see Chandni, you sleep.

Chandni is looking outside, Reyansh knocks her. and asks in sign language :

Reyansh : what happened?

Chandni ignores him and starts looking outside. After a while both of them fall asleep.

The flight lands in the morning. All three go to the hotel taxi. taxi driver Ali :

Ali : hello sir, welcome to Budapest.

Chhaiya : Indian……?

Ali : yes ma'am.

Aarav : Now let's go.

Everyone sits in the taxi. Reyansh also comes to take taxi from the same hotel.

Ali to all of them :

Ali : what is yours name?

Aarav : Aarav.

Chhaiya : Chhaiya.

Ali : and she Is Chandni?

All three were shock.

Chhaiya : how did you know?

Ali : am I right ?

Aarav : yes.

Ali :just guessed by the name of Chhaiya Ma'am.

Aarav : understand.

Chhaiya : what is your name?

Ali : My name is Ali, I am also the taxi driver of the hotel, and also travel around Budapest in my taxi.

Chhaiya : Means, you will be with us in our journey

Ali : yes ma'am.

Aarav : Are you stay with your family?

Tears start pouring out of Ali's eyes :

Aarav : are you crying?

Chhaiya : why are you crying?

Ali : Nope.

Aarav : then, this tears!

Ali : I have no one in this world, I am an orphan.

Both together : oooooooh, so sorry.

The Dark Moon

Ali wipes his tears and normally :

Ali : but it's okay, I have got used to it.

Chhaiya : So what was the need of doing so much drama?

Ali : Ma'am, when people like you give sympathy, then there is a feeling of belongingness.

Aarav : ooookay, We are yours, you are also from India, we are also from India, you are our.

Chhaiya : Brother, when will we reach the hotel?

Ali : brother……! It's about to arrive, sister.

Ali drives fast. Reyansh reaches the hotel while doing photography.

Ali's taxi reaches the hotel, all three go to the reception to get their room key, Reyansh also comes to collect his key at the same time, Chhaiya seeing her says to Chandni:

Chhaiya : Chandni, see over there.

Chandni : what!

Chhaiya : This is the man who was with you in the flight.

Chandni : hmmm.

Chhaiya : I think, he is also going to stay in this hotel.

Chandni : Aarav……!

Chhaiya : what happened Chandni? Why are you calling him?

Chandni : to tell him, you're seeing someone else instead of him.

Aarav comes :

Aarav : what happened ?

Chhaiya : nothing, you got the room key?

Aarav : yes I got, Chandni 3rd floor, room no. 319 is your room.

Chhaiya : and our?

Aarav : 322.

Chhaiya : okay.

Aarav : let's go, Takes rest for a while. Then see you for a lunch. Okay?

> All three go towards the lift. In sign language, Reyansh to receptionist :

Reyansh : room no.

Receptionist : room no?

Reyansh : yes.

Receptionist : 320.

> He moves towards the lift, the lift is about to stop, and she sees Reyansh running away, running away, she brings her foot to keep the lift open. Reyansh comes inside the lift.
>
> All forth reach the 3rd floor, everyone goes to their own room.
>
> Refreshing, Chandni goes to the balcony of her room, and she keeps looking at that beautiful view. At the same time, Reyansh comes to his balcony. He waves at her. Chandni ignores him and goes inside.
>
> Reyansh enjoys that beautiful view.
>
> Chhaiya and Aarav on the balcony:

Chhaiya : we did right?

The Dark Moon

Aarav : probably yes.

Chhaiya : We have taken her away from there, but what if her behavior does not change? then?

Aarav : Since when did you become negative, your role is positive.

Chhaiya : Aarav…..!

Aarav : don't worry, Everything will be fine, have you not heard that every morning brings a new hope, so a new place may have been taken with a new thought, We just have to leave her alone and be with her, understand?

Chhaiya : thank you.

Aarav : why?

Chhaiya : to help me.

Aarav looks down.

Chhaiya : what are you looking for?

Aarav : I see, if I throw you down here, only the bone is broken.

Chhaiya : Aarav….!

Aarav : shut up, she is my friend as well as yours, now let's take some rest, then has to go for lunch too.

Chhaiya : let's go.

    Both go inside the room.

    Everyone is having lunch together.

Ali came up :

Ali : Did you guys have lunch?

Chhaiya : Almost done, have you had your lunch?

Kahkashan Zaid

Ali : yes.
Aarav : good.

They finished their lunch :

Aarav : so shall we go?
Ali : let's go.

Ali takes those people around Budapest in his taxi. They were doing all the walking by stopping at one place. Chandni goes and sits near the sea. Chhaiya to Chandni:

Chhaiya : what happened Chandni? why have you sat over here?
Chandni : you guys enjoy, I want to sit over here for a while.
Aarav : okay......, but don't go anywhere from here!
Chandni : okay......

All three move on. Ali to both:

Ali : What happened to Chandni?
Chhaiya : nothing, Just want to take a sigh of relief.
Ali : oooh, over-pollution is also a problem in India.

Both starts laughing.

Reyansh is doing photography over there, he sees Chandni sitting in one place and takes a photo of her too. And smiles seeing her pictures :

Chandni is silently looking towards the sea.

Chhaiya and Aarav are walking together.

Aarav : What a beautiful place, isn't it!

The Dark Moon

Chhaiya : Literally.

          Suddenly Chhaiya started looking here and there.

Chhaiya : Where is Ali Bro?

Aarav : don't know.

          Meanwhile Ali came up to them :

Aarav : You were where?

Ali : Went to freshen up.

Both together : ooh.

Chhaiya : By the way, how many years have you been here?

Ali : I've been here for 8 years.

Aarav : 8 years....! You have been a taxi driver here for 8 years?

Ali : Yes and may be No!

Both together : means!

Ali : Earlier I used to do some other work, then started driving, in the earlier work, the money was less, so I started driving a taxi to the hotel.

Both together : ooooo hmmmm.

          Seeing this, he starts smiling.

Ali : you three are friends or.....!

Aarav : All three of us are friends, but me and Chhaiya are husband And wife.

Ali : You two so different and Chandni so calm, why?

Kahkashan Zaid

Chhaiya : The story is too long, tell you in a short story? Or tell the whole story?

Ali : I will listen the whole story another day, give a short story.

Chhaiya : You must know, how important is the color in the world, black complexions are considered bad and fair complexions are considered good, Whether there are people like me or people like Chandni, we all know how much we have to struggle with our Complexions, So just Chandni is also struggling with herself.

Ali : ooh, But you seem so confident, so why is she like this?

Chhaiya : I have got a lot of support from my Family, Chandni did not get any such support, so she takes more tension and gets anxious from all these things.

Ali says sadly.

Ali : The foundation of a person is his own people, when they are not together, it hurts a lot, family is important.

Seeing Ali sad, both console him.

Aarav : it's okay.

Chandni is sitting. A 7-year-old foreign child looks at her, he comes in front of her to see her, and smiles at her. Chandni gets nervous seeing him, and she sees the child laughing at her, she hears the same thing again. She starts running from there and

The Dark Moon

collides with Reyansh. She hugs Reyansh tight and starts crying. Reyansh puts his hand on his head lovingly and pats her.

After a while, Aarav Chhaiya and Ali go back to that Place, they do not see Chandni.

Aarav : where is Chandni!

Chhaiya : I told her, that doesn't go anywhere.

Aarav : call her.

Chhaiya : She doesn't have her phone!

Aarav Seriously says :

Aarav : So where is?

Chhaiya says nervously:

Chhaiya : Umm......, 319.

Aarav : Means?

Chhaiya : hotel room, She has left her phone at the hotel room.

Aarav shouts :

Aarav : What......! So, she should have been a hotel herself too, we are not in our country, we are somewhere else, the phone should be with us, isn't it?

Ali : clam down, It is better to get angry than to seek her, let's go a little further and see, maybe we will find her, the place is new for her, she may not have gone too far.

Both together : let's go.

As Chandni is sitting on a seat, Reyansh brings water for her. He gives her water to drink, Chandni is dull. Reyansh asks her to drink water with the sign language. Chandni drinks water with understanding. Then she tells him.

Chandni : why are you behaving like this? I mean why are you not speaking?

Reyansh in sign language :

Reyansh : I cannot speak.

Chandni gets shocked seeing this.

Chandni : You cannot speak!

Reyansh : Yes.

At the same time, all three come looking for her.

Ali : See over there, Chandni is there!

Chhaiya : Let's go.

All three came up to her.

Chhaiya : Chandni....! Are you fine?

Aarav : Why did you come here from there?

Chhaiya : Chandni, How tense were we?

Reyansh says quickly in sign language, all three do not understand.

Ali : Who is he? And what is he trying to say?

Chandni : actually he can not speak.

Chandni says to Reyansh :

Chandni : thank you for helping me.

Chhaiya : thank you for taking care of her.

The Dark Moon

And from there everyone starts leaving, Chandni looks at him, and Reyansh sees her with smiling and waves. Chandni moves on.

Chandni is sitting on her balcony at night, thinking about Reyansh. Meanwhile, Saanvi calls Chandni, she disconnects the call in the mist of anger and starts thinking about Reyansh again.

Chhaiya to Saanvi on phone :

Chhaiya : Aunty why are you getting Anxious! She is absolutely fine.

Saanvi : Since when have I been calling her, she is not picking up the call.

Chhaiya : Okay...., we are going for dinner, I will tell her to call you, okay......?

Saanvi : okay... dear.

Phone cut:

Viraj : What she is saying?

Saanvi : she will tell her to call me after dinner.

Aarav to Chhaiya :

Aarav : what happened?

Chhaiya : Chandni doesn't pick up her parent's call.

Aarav : She's probably still upset with them.

Chhaiya : hmmm may be.

Aarav : let's go for dinner.

Chhaiya : let's go.

The four are having lunch together. Ali to all three :

Kahkashan Zaid

Ali : thank you very much, guys.

Chhaiya : for what?

Ali : You are feeding a driver like me with you in the hotel.

Aarav : Hey Ali brother, what are you talking about, we are your own people, and are eaten by sitting with loved ones.

Everyone is having their dinner, at the same time Chandni's eyes fall on Reyansh, he is having dinner sitting alone. Chandni continues to stare at him, as Reyansh looks at her, she lowers her eyes. Reyansh goes to all of them. He takes permission from them to sit.

Aarav : Yes, please.

Reyansh sign language me :

Reyansh : She was watching me from here, so I came here.

Chandni understands, and the three starts seeing each other's faces.

Ali : Chandni did something with you?

Reyansh : No.......

Cisndni is nervous :

Chandni : Can we have our dinner? Silently!

Everyone having their dinner. After dinner:

Aarav : Let's go out to eat ice cream.

Ali : I am going home, I am used to sleeping early.

The Dark Moon

Aarav : Okay, Chandni You?

Chandni : You two go, I'm not fond of becoming a bone in a kebab.

Aarav Reyansh se :

Aarav : ooh sorry, we didn't ask your name, your name?

> Reyansh writes his name and give to him.

Aarav : Reyansh, and I am Aarav, she is my wife Chhaiya, She is our friend Chandni and he is our brother Ali Bro.

Ali : I am the driver of this hotel, now I must go, okay bye.

All together : bye

> Ali left from there. Chhaiya asks Reyansh:

Chhaiya : Reyansh what do you do?

> Reyansh shows his business card :

Aarav : You're a businessman! you can't speak then!

Chandni : Business is done with the mind, not with the tongue.

Chhaiya to Reyansh :

Chhaiya : Are you in the habit of sleeping early?

Reyansh : nope.

Chhaiya : So you would like to go for a walk outside with Chandni?

> Chandni started looking at Chhaiya angrily:

Chhaiya : see, she is telling me thank you in her eyes.

> Chandni is looking at her in surprise.

~ 69 ~

Kahkashan Zaid

Chhaiya : All right let's go, you both go too, bye.

> Chhaiya quickly grabs Aarav's hand and leaves quickly from there. Reyansh and Chandni are looking at each other's faces.
>
> Chhaiya comes out laughing.

Aarav : what you've done?

> She was just laughing. After a while, while walking on the road :

Aarav : If you have calmed down now, then tell me why you did this, you made Reyansh with Chandni! Why?

Chhaiya : I saw twice today that Chandni keeps looking at Reyansh.

Aarav : When?

Chhaiya : The first time, when we met him for the first time, and the second time, when we were having dinner, that's why he came to sit with us there.

Aarav : You are trying to say this to Chandni and Reyansh.......!

Chhaiya : I don't know that, but I feel like.

Aarav : I don't understand anything, what are you saying?

Chhaiya : First take ice cream, then cool the mind and listen to me.

Both take ice cream.

Chhaiya : How's the ice cream?

Aarav : delicious, now tell me.

The Dark Moon

Both sit on the seat   :

Chhaiya : You know, what is the biggest flaw in all of us humans?

Aarav   : What! Umm...

Chhaiya : Okay. You know what is the deficiency in you?

Aarav   : of course I know.

Chhaiya : tell me.

Aarav   : I do not understand many things quickly, and I am very upset about this thing, why did God give me this lack, why he didn't give me something else?

Chhaiya laughing at him

Aarav   : don't laugh at me, I am your husband.

Chhaiya Normally   :

Chhaiya : How did you feel when I laughed at you?

Aarav   : I felt like, I'm so dumb.

Chhaiya : You have a lack of confidence, take 2 times confidence in the morning and the evening.

Aarav   : Chhaiya......!

Chhaiya : Let all that go, I want to tell you that you have a lack of understanding, and in me, people can be seen, but why are we both together, because...

Aarav   : we love each other.

Chhaiya : Exactly, Reyansh can't speak but he is a big businessman, and as Chandni said, business needs a brain not a tongue, He put his ability in front of his biggest shortcoming, he doesn't have a voice, so what happened, God has given his brain in abundance, Hands are not needed to become a writer, this Nick Vujicic from Australia proved, God took hands and feet, But gave a good thought by which he motivates others with his words, No need of Foot to run away, this Shalini Saraswathi from India proved, Despite having no legs, became India's best blade runner, There are shortcomings in everyone, know them and focus on your ability.

Aarav becomes shock :

Chhaiya : What happened to you now?

Aarav : You did mass media, didn't you?

Chhaiya : yes but, why are you asking?

Aarav : You talked like a philosopher.

Chhaiya Started laughing :

Chhaiya : Some moments of life make you a Philosopher, everyone is a Philosopher in their lives, now let's walk a little.

Aarav : Let's go Mrs. philosopher.

Both walking together :

Chandni and Reyansh were walking. Both are walking silently, Chandni in her mind:

Chandni : What did this Chhaiya do, what should I talk about, he will not speak anything, and what should I say, I do not understand anything.

The Dark Moon

       Chandni is nervous and tries to talk to him.

Chandni : umm. …., Are you dumb since childhood?

Chandni in her mind :

Chandni : what am I saying?

       Reyansh in sign language :

Reyansh : small.

Chandni : Childhood?

Reyansh : Yes, What do you do?

Chandni : Me?

Reyansh : Yes.

Chandni : I studied mass media, but no one give me the job because….

Reyansh : what are you doing here?

Chandni : Here! I am here……!

Chandni in her mind :

Chandni : what should I say?

Reyansh knocks her.

Chandni : I am here for some rest.

Reyansh : same.

       Both are walking, and both of them see a small child. Both go to that child, Reyansh tries to talk to him with his sign language, but the small child starts screaming.

Chandni : let me try.

Chandni to Sameer :

Chandni : what happened? Why are you crying over here? And where are your parents?

Sameer is crying, and after a while, Sameer is eating ice cream. Meanwhile, his parents came up to him :

Sameera and Abdullah are a Muslim couple, Sameera is like Chandni, A dark complexion and Abdullah is like Reyansh, he can't speak.

Sameera : Sameer!

Sameera Start kissing him.

Abdullah is dumb, Reyansh and Abdullah keep looking at each other.

Chandni : you?

Sameera : Sameera his mother.

Chandni : ooh, and he?

Sameera : Abdullah his father.

Chandni : ooh, where were you guys?

Sameera : I don't know when, but he let go of my hand.

Chandni : It's ok, it happens sometimes.

Sameera : you?

Chandni : I am Chandni from India.

Sameera : I am also from India.

Chandni : ooh, nice to meet you.

Sameera : nice to meet you too.

Chandni : Your husband doesn't like to talk?

Sameera : He cannot speak, and he?

Chandni : he too.

Sameera And Chandni look at them.

The Dark Moon

After a while, all while eating ice cream. Reyansh and Abdullah are laughing and talking to each other. Sameera looks at both of them and says.

Sameera : How happy are both of them?

Chandni : hmmm.

Chandni continuously looks at her. Sameera asks Chandni :

Sameera : What happened to you?

Chandni : can I ask you something?

Sameera : please……

Chandni : you and him? How?

Sameera : if I am not wrong, you must be thinking that me and Abdullah like you and Reyansh, right?

Chandni : Maybe.

Sameera : your eyes telling, me that you struggled a lot with your complexion, am I right or wrong?

Chandni : you also struggled.

Sameera : Wherever you are, I have passed from there, I belong to a Muslim family, Where girls are taught veils after an age, and our veils are covered with black clothes, so I used to ask my mother, I'm so dark, why do I need a veil? So, you know what did she answer?

Chandni : What!

Sameera : Everyone is in love with the black Kaaba and everyone is afraid of the white shroud, And also that every girl has her own beauty, and

Kahkashan Zaid

          the veil belongs to that beauty, Allah has bestowed all the girls with her beauty, and every girl is beautiful, no matter what kind of complexion they have.

Chandni : Beautiful people are those, people whose complexion is fair, dark people like us only work as a stain in the moon, Black people like us are that stain in the moon, which no one likes to see.

Sameera Smiling :

Sameera : Look at that moon.

Both starts looking toward the moon.

Chandni : How beautiful it is, shining.

Sameera : But what will be the status of this moon, if it shines in the light?

Chandni looks at her, and says surprisingly :

Chandni : What......!

Sameera : What, what, answer my question.

Chandni : If a shining thing shines in the light, then its value......

Sameera : Similarly, the moon looks beautiful to a person only when it comes out in the dark of night, not in the light of day, The moon needs darkness to shine, the darkness does not need the moon, or you may say both need both.

          Hearing this, Chandni's mind starts to open up.

The Dark Moon

Sameera : You know, what is the issue with people like us? Of our thinking, if someone in us says that we are very black, then we feel bad, Why can't we be happy, if we are black then we are black, what is the harm in believing ourselves? When they can be happy to call fair as fair, then what is the harm in calling black as black? You must be feeling that I am sweeping the philosophy, but this philosophy also took a long time to be formed, I have lost a lot of good people in this complexion war, don't you make this mistake, can I give you a piece of advice?

Chandni : yes please.

Sameera : Whenever you see someone smile, then smile at them, and when someone smiles, hug them, this is what Abdullah taught me.

Chandni : My friend Chhaiya also does this thing, but what is the difference between the two?

Sameera : There is a big difference, people laugh at you when they are making fun of you, And smiling is when they are happy to see you, I hope these words of mine have helped you, Taking my words seriously, life is only one, one wrong step will give lifelong regret.

Chandni : I am feeling very good.

Sameera : And you asked, that I and Abdullah?

Chandni : How?

Kahkashan Zaid

Sameera : Because we respect, love, and understand each other more than ourselves, love is such a thing, which does not see any boundaries.

Chandni : You both look good together.

Sameera : Reyansh and you will look good together.

Chandni : Now I have to think about it.

Sameera : Don't think, make what is yours, sit down to think, so a lot of time will be wasted.

Both start smiling :

Sameera and Chandni goes to both of them :

Sameera : Abdullah! Let's go?

Sameera Abdullah and Sameer greeting Chandni and Reyansh

Chandni : bye.

Sameera : bye.

> Reyansh and Chandni are walking, Chandni is very happy, she is smiling remembering Sameera's words.

Reyansh knock her :

Reyansh : What happened? You looking so happy.

Chandni : You are in sleepy mood?

Reyansh : Nope.

Chandni : Then let's go.

Reyansh : Where?

Chandni : Just come with me.

The Dark Moon

>Both go to the park, both roam there a lot, Chandni clicks pictures on her phone, both enjoy a lot.

Chhaiya and Aarav vacate outside the hotel. Chhaiya in tension :

Chhaiya : Where is this girl, earlier she did not want to go, now she is not taking the name of coming, and when I am calling, she is not even picking up the phone.

Aarav : Relax, both of them are not children, they will come.

Chhaiya : I feel that Reyansh has done it.

Aarav Angrily :

Aarav : What's the matter with you girls? You start thinking of every boy as a cruel rogue, you saw his face, how innocent he is, why are you spoiling his image?

Chhaiya : Why she is not picking up my phone?

Aarav : I'll tell you by asking.

Chhaiya Angrily staring at him.

Aarav : sorry.

>Meanwhile, Chandni send her and Reyansh happy face pictures. Chhaiya seeing all those pictures, she shock and at the same time happily says :

Chhaiya : oh my God!

Aarav : What happened?

Chhaiya : see.

Aarav   : What?

Aarav and Chhaiya seeing those pictures together, and says happily :

Aarav   : your plan worked.

Chhaiya : yeah....., I am so happy for her, But how all this so fast?

Aarav   : Leave all that, she is happy, this is enough for us, that was the purpose of our coming here, and it seems to be being fulfilled.

Chhaiya : yes, but why she don't picking up my call?

Aarav   : don't disturb them, enjoy them their own time.

Chhaiya : I think you are right.

Aarav   : I am always right.

Chhaiya : ooh.

Chhaiya ignores him and goes inside the hotel. Aarav says irritatedly   :

Aarav   : she doesn't respect me, I am so cool and smart, by the way, I am not smart, but cool enough, I am always right.

And happily goes inside the hotel.

Chandni and Reyansh are sitting by the sea, Chandni smiles happily and takes a long breath, seeing this, Reyansh is also happy, and says :

Reyansh knock her :

Chandni : hmmm!

Reyansh : You look great when you smile.

The Dark Moon

Chandni : thank you.

Reyansh : But how are you suddenly so happy?

Chandni : Aaaaah, I don't understand!

Reyansh tries to understand her slowly :

Reyansh : You.

Chandni : Hmmm, me!

Reyansh : Why are you so happy?

Chandni : Why I am so happy?

Reyansh : Yes.

Chandni : Because I am not the only person who is facing all these things.

> Reyansh had no idea what Chandni was talking about. Chandni Says Smiley :

Chandni : Didn't understand anything?

Reyansh : Nope.

Chandni : Like to hear the story?

Reyansh : Yes.

Chandni smiling :

Chhaiya thinks while drinking coffee while standing on the balcony of her room :

Chhaiya : I am happy for Chandni, but this happiness should not be temporary, this world is full of bastard thoughts, here man is happy, but people have made him a sad soul again by talking wrong things. I hope Chandni is happy for whatever reason, he should always be with her.

> Meanwhile, Aarav came up to her:

Kahkashan Zaid

Aarav : What are you thinking about?

Chhaiya : You know, when Chandni and I met for the first time, she was just like me, just like I was before, unconfident, no one cares, we became each other's first friends, I knew Whenever someone in us said black and white, she used to get upset, and because of the same thing, there was a rift in our friendship. But today I am getting the same feelings for Chandni, Reyansh and she is very different in appearance when people see them together, then say something wrong, and then Chandni will break down.

Aarav : You know why I love you so much?

Chhaiya : Because you did not get anybody.

Aarav : Of course.

Chhaiya : What did you say?

Aarav laughing:

Aarav : I'm kidding, I had a friend, who is no more, he died at the age of 9.

Chhaiya : Hawwww, so sad.

Aarav : He was also like you, we all friends used to call him White Ghost before, he was all alone, he never used to talk to anyone, But his nature towards people, he was also like you, overall you seemed to me like another Advik, but he was not confident like you, But I don't know why, I felt like I should be friends with him, and I also made him my friend, then I realized he is not a white ghost,

The Dark Moon

he is a white angel, He had said one thing to me, it is better to make fun of someone's lack than ever, to appreciate his talent, it is better to find fault in someone, Find good in him, it will increase the confidence of that person, his words gave me the feeling that I am talking to a 9 not but 90-year-old man, Now tell me how big will his trouble be.

Chhaiya : Can't say so much, to talk deeply, it is necessary to have a wound in the surroundings.

Aarav : If Reyansh was interested in Chandni, then he would not agree to go on a walk with her, even though he was very happy, I feel, seeing both of them happy, that now Chandni has really shone.

Chhaiya, happily :

Chhaiya : hope so.

Aarav : hope so.

Chhaiya : By the way, how did your friend die?

Aarav : Whom friend?

Chhaiya : What you were just talking about, Advik!

Aarav : him?

Chhaiya : yes, him.

Aarav : I had just come after watching a movie, so this story was formed in my mind, So I just tell you the small story.

Chhaiya : One minute, That 9 90 was this your story?

Aarav : Yes.

Chhaiya looks at Aarav angrily, Aarav gets nervous, Chhaiya runs to kill him, Aarav runs away, and pitches to Chhaiya.

Chhaiya : How bad are you, said as if everything is true.

Aarav : See, I said very nice words.

Chhaiya : By creating such a sad scene, you are saying that there was a story!

Aarav : But think about how good the story was.

Chhaiya looks at him angrily, he comes running inside the room, Chhaiya runs after him and beats him by throwing the pillow.

Aarav : Chhaiya! How can you beat me, I am your husband.

Chhaiya : Husband!

Chhaiya beats him by throwing another pillow, both of them start a pillow fight, the whole room becomes rueful. Both start laughing, and love each other very much.

Chandni to Reyansh:

Chandni : Today Sameera changed my thinking, and explained me a lot things, and explained the biggest thing, that I am not alone, there are many people like me.

Reyansh smiles. Chandni smiling:

Chandni : You must be thinking, how talkative I am!

Reyansh : I can't speak, but I can hear, maybe that's why God took away my voice and made me able to hear, so that I can hear your words.

The Dark Moon

She doesn't understand anything.

Chandni : Did not understand anything, but you must have said something good.

Both start laughing :

The happy days on.

Ali travels to Budapest with four of them, Reyansh also clicks everyone's pictures with his camera, and everyone enjoys it a lot. Having dinner together, going for a walk outside after dinner, and eating ice cream in Budapest in the cold, Chandni really started living life.

Aarav says irritated while having lunch:

Aarav : Oh man......, I am tired of eating hotel food, I am not feeling well now.

Chhaiya : It's true, the taste that food, is it not in hotel food!

Ali : So you guys eat dinner tonight at my house!

Chandni : Yours house!

Ali : I know, you guys like me in the house of a driver.

Aarav : No filmy dialogues, we will come, and you will make biryani for us.

Everyone together : yes.

Ali happily:

Ali : for sure, I will feed you the world's best biryani.

~ 85 ~

Kahkashan Zaid

Chandni : wow biryani, we will have to starve from now on.

Everyone laughing :

Chhaiya : But we will also help you.

Ali : There is no need for that, Allah has given me this ability, that I can be the hospitality of you people.

Reyansh : But sweet dish from our side.

Everyone starts looking towards Chandni:

Chandni : sweet dish from our side.

Aarav : You will not refuse it.

Ali : Umm..... okay, Let's meet at night's feast.

Everyone together : ok bye.

Ali : bye.

Ali left there. Chhaiya to everyone :

Chhaiya : How sweet Ali bro!

Aarav : Literally.

Reyansh : Why don't we get some gifts for him today?

Aarav and Chhaiya, after seeing him, look at Chandni, Chandni to both of them:

Chandni : One minute.

Chandni to Reyansh :

Chandni : what are you trying to say? easily explain?

Reyansh tries to understand her slowly, Chandni understands the matter, then smiles at both of them and says:

Chandni : He is saying that we take some gifts for him?

Aarav happily :

Aarav : it's a good idea.

Chhaiya : Literally! But what….?

Chandni : Let's go there, and decide over there.

    Ali was engaged in the preparation of the feast, taking all the ingredients from the market, he prepares to make biryani.

    And on the other hand, four of them go to the shopping mall to get gifts for him. Chhaiya and Chandni are roaming in the shopping mall, Chhaiya sees something in a shop, which she is very happy to see, She to Chandni :

Chhaiya : Chandni……!

Chandni : hmmm….

Chhaiya : See over there.

    Both of them see each other smiling after seeing that thing.

    Aarav and Reyansh are walking together, Aarav sees a nice thing, and he knocks Reyansh. Both of them look at that thing, smiling at each other.

    After some time, Chandni and Chhaiya are having coffee in the cafeteria, Aarav and Reyansh come to both of them with coffee, looking at the bags in their hands.

Chhaiya : Shopping is done.

Aarav : Yes.

Chandni : Why do you both have so many bags?

Reyansh : You guys also have bags.

Aarav : You guys also have bags.

Both sit and drink coffee.

Chandni and Chhaiya are surprised:

Chhaiya : Do you understand what he said?

Aarav : No, I spoke my words! Look in the hands of you people, we have only 4 bags in our hands, both of you look at yourself!

Aarav counts the bags of both.

Aarav : 4 4 8, you both have 4 4 bags in your hand, and you are telling us.

Chandni Smiling:

Chandni : Well you are Such a little kid, we are girls, come to the shopping mall, do not do shopping, this can never happen.

Reyansh : What gifts did you purchase?

Chandni : Gifts?

Reyansh : Yes.

Chandni : I purchased a watch and Chhaiya.....

Chhaiya : I purchased a bracelet.

Reyansh starts seeing Aarav in anger, Aarav gets nervous and starts looking at Reyansh at the rate, seeing both of them as like this, Chandni and Chhaiya look at each other. Chandni to Reyansh:

Chandni : What happened? Why are you looking at him like this?

The Dark Moon

Aarav in Nervousness :

Aarav : Ummmm.

Chhaiya : what ummmm, Say something further.

Aarav : actually, we both also purchased the same things, and he told me through message, that I ask You, what they are purchasing, but I didn't listen to him.

    Chandni and Chhaiya look at each other in surprise, then start laughing out loud. Reyansh is still staring at Aarav, and Aarav is hiding his eyes from him.

    Aarav is angry with both of them :

Aarav : Why are you both laughing?

Chandni : Aarav…..! Are you really still mad?

Aarav : Chandni……!

Chhaiya : We have not taken the watch nor the bracelet, we know what both of you have purchased.

Reyansh : How?

Chandni : because you both have brand names on your bags, that's why.

    Both of them start looking at their bags. Chandni and Chhaiya start laughing again. Chandni suddenly sees the same child again, who is smiling looking at her near the sea. The child is still smiling looking at her. Chandni remembers Sameera's words. She goes to that child. Seeing Her leaving, Chhaiya says :

Chhaiya : Chandni! Chandni! Where she is going?

> All three go after her. Chandni goes to him fast, as soon as she comes near him, she slowly comes to him. He was still looking at her smiling. Chandni very calmly asks him:

Chandni : why are you smiling?

Kid : because you are the most beautiful woman.

> Chandni smiles on hearing this and Chhaiya, Aarav, and Reyansh are happy.

Kid : you have a phenomenal smile and beautiful eyes.

> The child kisses her on the chicks and runs away from there.
>
> Chandni had tears in her eyes and a smile on her lips.
>
> Chandni is sitting alone in front of the sea, she is remembering the words of that child, and she is happy.
>
> She tells herself in her mind :

Chandni : I wish I would take Chhaiya's words seriously, she always motivated me with her words, and tried to building confidence in me, And what I did with her, Reyansh in my life is also because of her, where I am today only because of her.

> Reyansh comes and stands beside her, Chandni gives him a place to sit, he sits, Chandni rests his head on his shoulder, she

The Dark Moon

holds his hand, and takes a sigh of relief, and closes her eyes.

After 10 seconds of closing her eyes, someone comes there, hearing whose voice Chandni opens her eyes, and she is shocked to see them.

It's evening. Aarav and Reyansh leave from their rooms wearing kurta pajama. Aarav to Reyansh:

Aarav : You are looking very handsome, and the color is also suiting you.

Reyansh is wearing a bottle green kurta pajama, and Aarav is wearing a navy blue color.

Reyansh : Looks good on you too.

Aarav Happily :

Aarav : Looking good on me!

Reyansh : Yes.

Aarav : thank you, Where are these two girls, we are getting late!

Chhaiya and Chandni both leave from Chandni's room, Chandni is wearing bottle green and Chhaiya is wearing a navy blue anarkali, And both of them come very well ready, when they see both Aarav and Reyansh, they keep on seeing them, Seeing the color of both Chhaiya and Chandni, they are surprised.

Chhaiya : Same same!

Chandni : yeah.....

Aarav : Both of you have taken the same color as us, Chhaiya, you are looking gorgeous.

Chhaiya : Thank you, you are also looking very good.

Reyansh looking at Chandni :

Reyansh : Looking Gorgeous.

Chandni : You too.

> The two hold their hands in each other's hands, and leave for Ali's house.
>
> Chhaiya Chandni and Reyansh are in the back seat and Aarav is in the seat next to the driver's seat. Chandni was thinking something sitting in the taxi, she was a bit upset, Chhaiya seeing her like this and asks her :

Chhaiya : What happened Chandni? what are you thinking?

Aarav and Reyansh also start seeing her. Chandni Normally says :

Chandni : Nothing, I am just thinking, what to purchase for sweet dish?

Aarav : Oh yes, we forgot it.

> Aarav taxi driver says :

Aarav : Driver, please stop the taxi at some nice sweet shop!

Driver : okay sir.

> Chandni starts thinking again, Reyansh holds her hand and sees her smiling.

The Dark Moon

           Ali is waiting desperately for four of them outside in his house, in his own voice:

Ali : The location was sent to these people, where have they remained till now? I call them.

           As soon as he gets the phone out of the pocket, at the same time those people come there, four of them get down from the taxi.

Ali : Where did you all stuck?

           Ali happily seeing four of them in a Muslim traditional dress and says :

Ali : Mashallah, You all look so nice!

Four of them : Thank you so much.

Ali : let's go inside.

Aarav : let's go.

           Ali brings four of them inside his house.

Ali : Look, this is my house, my little house.

           Ali's house is very small, but a beautiful house, he made them sit and welcomed them.

Chandni : your house is small but it is very beautiful, you maintain very well.

           Ali smiles.

           Everyone gives gifts to Ali.

Chhaiya : We have brought something for you, please accept it.

           Seeing the gifts, Ali says :

Ali : There is no need for all this.

Chandni : It is necessary that you will remember all these things in us later.

          Hearing this, Ali could not say anything, and silently he took the gift from them.

Ali : Thank you all so much.

Aarav : Thank you, the biryani's smell is very loud, now there is no patience.

          Everyone starts laughing after listening to Aarav's words.

          Ali laid Dastarkhan in a very beautiful way, in all this Chhaiya and Chandni helped him, and dinner started.

          Everyone starts eating biryani, Ali is waiting for everyone's reaction, everyone tastes biryani and starts watching Ali seriously. He gets nervous seeing everyone's faces, and asks :

Ali : What happened? Biryani is not tasty?

          Everyone smiles seeing him, and says :

Reyansh : best.

Chandni : very tasty.

Chhaiya : Wonderful.

          Aarav pays attention to the food and enjoys the biryani.

Ali : How did you like Aarav?

          He is still enjoying Biryani, Chhaiya to Aarav:

The Dark Moon

Chhaiya : Aarav! Aarav! Ali bro is asking something to you.

Aarav : I will not waste time in telling, I will focus only on the food.

Everyone starts laughing after listening to Aarav.

Chhaiya : mad.

Everyone having their dinner very slightly. Chandni is wondering something while dinner, Chhaiya saw her, and telling in herself in her mind :

Chhaiya : there is something mess, what she is thinking? In the taxi she was also thinking!

And she having her dinner.

After dinner. Chhaiya is worried about Chandni, she constantly thinking about what she is thinking. Ali saw her, and asks her :

Ali : Chhaiya?

She doesn't answer

Ali : Chhaiya?

Chhaiya : yes?

Ali : what are you thinking?

Everyone looking at her :

Chhaiya : Nothing!

Ali : nope, there is something wrong.

Aarav came up to her :

Aarav : What happened Chhaiya? Everything is alright?

Chandni : Chhaiya! there is something bothering you?

Chhaiya start acting, that she is hiding something to them :

Chhaiya : I am not going to tell you at least.

Everyone get confuse.

Chandni : Why are you talking like this?

Chhaiya : Why I can't ?

Chandni : I am your friend, best friend, Best friend share problems to each other.

Chhaiya goes to her, she put her hands on her shoulders, and says very politely:

Chhaiya : exactly my darling, if you not share your problem with me, then why are you expecting from me.

Chandni constantly looking at her. Everyone looking at each other.

Sea view : Chandni and Reyansh sat on the chairs and holds their hands. Ananya saw Chandni.

Ananya : Is She Chandni?

she goes towards them and says loudly:

Ananya : hey Darky.

Chandni and Reyansh open their eyes, and when saw her she gets shocked.

Chandni : Ananya you?

Ananya : I surprised you, isn't?

The Dark Moon

        Chandni gets nervous. Ananya saw Reyansh and asks to her:

Ananya : who is he?

Chandni gets more nervous, meanwhile, Reyansh holds her hand, Chandni looks at him. Ananya says seriously :

Ananya : he is your boyfriend?

        Reyansh shakes his head. Ananya started laughing at them. And says :

Ananya : you two like how? Chandni You have seen yourself, and look at him, just like the moon with the stain.

Chandni gets nervous, her hands start trembling, Reyansh holds her hand, and gives courage to her with his eyes. Ananya says in very negative attitude :

Ananya : You look at yourself, you were black and you are still black, And look at me, it was beautiful and today I am more beautiful, we have not changed at all.

        Reyansh angrily tells him very badly in sign language. Ananya is shocked to see him, and asks Chandni with a Laugh :

Ananya : Is he dumb?

        She laugh badly at Reyansh and calmly she says to Chandni :

Ananya : That's what I think, how did you get such a handsome man.

Chandni gets very angry after hearing all this, then she remembers Sameera's words.

Chandni's attitude change. She faces Ananya with her eyes raised. Ananya laughs, Chandni walks closer to her.

Ananya : What happened? Feeling bad?

Chandni is looking at her seriously, then suddenly starts smiling, Ananya gets confused :

Chandni : Nope, not at all, but I agree with you on one thing, don't you want to ask?

Ananya : Which?

Chandni : we both have not changed till today, you were beautiful and today you are even more beautiful, I was black and am still black, but one more thing hasn't changed, Your beauty is high, but your mentality is still low.

Hearing this, Ananya gets angry.

Ananya : What did you say....

Chandni : What happened? felt bad.......

Ananya : you...

Chandni : What happened? There is nothing to say.

Ananya : You probably don't know, I work in TV news.

Chandni : I know everything, it is the job of your channel to spread false news, maybe people watch that channel because of your beauty, and listen to the news, but what does it matter to salable reporters like you, what kind of news are you putting on air?

The Dark Moon

Ananya : When you worked there, you would have come to know how pressurized we people are.

Chandni : As far as I know there will be no such compulsion in your house, that you have to earn money by lying.

Ananya : When you are the idol of so much truth, why would you be reporting?

Chandni's tongue closes :

Ananya : What happened! The snake got bitten by the tongue? It is easy to say many things, but more difficult to do, and I think, You would not have been allowed to give an interview just by looking at your face if They started giving jobs to a black girl like you with TV news, No one has come to see any news on that channel, no one likes to see a blot on their channel.

Ananya calmly says :

Ananya : Maybe for today this lesson will be useful for you.

And starts going from there. Chandni says from behind him :

Chandni : Someday you will come to this Kali.

Ananya : And for what?

When you come, you will know that.

Ananya : That day never comes.

Chandni : Surely come.

Ananya comes closer to her :

Ananya : What did you do? Will you report yourself or....

Chandni : Wait and watch, now this moon will shine, you know "the dark moon".

Both keep looking into each other's eyes.

Ananya : will see.

Chandni : will see.

Ananya leaves from there. After she is gone, Chandni and Reyansh keep looking at each other.

Present time :

Everyone is sitting silently looking at the moonlight. Chhaiya is giving compliment Chandni on her shoulder:

Chhaiya : Confident.....

Aarav shouts :

Aarav : over confident.

Everyone was looking at him.

Aarav : You girls are really unpredictable, if you are not confident, then you remain silent, and suddenly say anything confidently.

Chhaiya : Aarav shut up, she didn't do anything wrong. Don't know how she is speaking, why are you intimidating her?

Chandni : He is right, in anger, I may have challenged her!

Reyansh puts his hand on her shoulder. Ali to Chandni :

The Dark Moon

Ali : This is another good thing, some challenges show you your new look.

Chhaiya : Means?

Ali : Nothing is achieved without any difficulties, some mistakes in life are for the good, you have challenged it, so you have completed it.

Chandni : But how…..?

Ali : That's something to think about.

Everyone starts thinking, and Reyansh starts writing something on a book and paper. Aarav looking at her asks :

Aarav : what are you writing?

Everyone starts looking toward Reyansh. After he writes the paper, he gives the paper to Chandni. Chandni reads the paper to loudly :

Chandni : After reading the whole paper, give your reaction, you become a reporter, a report that you own, your decisions, your rules, Where you don't need anyone's permission, to tell the truth, where you can't pressurize anyone to tell a lie.

Hearing this, everyone starts looking at Reyansh. Chhaiya happily being aware of this :

Chhaiya : This is a very good idea, if we only want to tell the truth, then this is a very good idea.

Chandni : But, who will see us?

Aarav : There are people in this world who value listening to the truth and those who tell the truth, and nowadays more children are on the phone, And nowadays more children are on the phone, if we tell the truth to them then they will definitely support us, instead of our truth, we will get their support.

Chandni : But.....

Everyone shouts together: But what....?

Chandni : Nothing

After 2 days. At the Airport, 4ro Ali se:

Chandni : To see us have a good time here.

Ali : Thank you guys for showing me a good time.

Aarav : Funny things are, ache din to hasn't come yet but you have definitely seen a good time.

Everyone starts laughing. From Ali Chhaiya and Chandni :

Ali : I will pray that Allah gives you both a lot of courage, and to face every truth, the path is very difficult, But the difficulties of both of you will create ease for a lot of people.

Together : Thank you.

Aarav : Now we should go inside.

Reyansh and Rao say goodbye to Ali, and the 4 rowers go inside. Ali waves Four of them and tears well in his eyes. Four of them also wave to him and go inside. After going inside those people. Ali looked up and raised his hand to Allah :

The Dark Moon

Ali	: By helping these people, and creating a new mindset, Ameen…..

And from there, it goes.

They land in India:

Reyansh goes to his house in his car and all three reach Chandni's house, Chhaiya gets down of the taxi and Aarav goes inside, Chandni keeps watching Divya's house from the gate of her house. Saanvi is cooking food and Viraj is working on the new paper. Chhaiya and Aarav come in.

Chhaiya	: hello uncle!

Viraj gets surprised to see both of them and says :

Viraj	: Whom Chandni Aarav, you guys have come?
Aarav	: Are we invisible?

All three start laughing. Viraj loudly call Saanvi :

Viraj	: Saanvi look who has come.

Saanvi comes out of the kitchen and looks happy but does not see Chandni and asks both :

Saanvi	: Chandni didn't come?

Viraj looking behind both :

Viraj	: Yes, Chandni didn't come along?
Aarav	: she Was with us just now.

Kahkashan Zaid

               Chandni claps quietly at the gate of Divya's house, then swings at the gate with a smile, and shouts to Divya :

Chandni : Divyaaaaaaa Auntyyyyyyyyy.

               Saanvi, Viraj, Chhaiya and Aarav hear 4 voices.

Saanvi : What is she doing outside?

Viraj : Let's see.

               Four of them go out towards the outside of the house. Divya comes outside her house.

Divya : Uh.... you have come, and why are you calling me?

               Chandni just keeps smiling looking at Divya. Seeing Chandni swinging at the gate, Divya angrily goes to her and says :

Divya : First, get down from the gate, will break the gate!

               Chandni descends from the gate. At the same time Four of them come up to Chandni :

Saanvi : Chandni! what are you doing here?

Chandni : Mother, today a very old account has to be settled.

Divya : What....?

               Chandni slowly moves towards Divya, and very calmly says :

Chandni : Auntie you are very beautiful, your kids will be like you too, right?

The Dark Moon

Divya happily :

Divya : Everyone has gone to me.

Chandni : Let's assume, I have not even seen it till today, where are your children?

Divya : Everyone is shifting out with their family, it has been many years, and I have not even seen them.

Chandni : You tell me really one thing, to amuse your heart, you call me bad, don't you?

Divya was shocked to hear this. Chandni hugs Divya and says lovingly :

Chandni : I am not fair like you but I am definitely your daughter, who was always with you.

Hearing this, tears welled up in Divya's eyes and Chandni happily says :

Chandni : And you can rightfully call me dark, I don't mind at all.

Everyone is very happy to see this positive attitude. Divya kisses Chandni on the chick and holds her nose and says :

Divya : My darling darky.

Everyone starts laughing. Divya is hugging Chandni.

It is night, Chandni is sitting on the Rakhi chair in front of the study table in her room and is talking to Reyansh on a video call on his laptop, At the same time Saanvi comes

Kahkashan Zaid

there, sees Chandni talking to the boy, Saanvi asks in surprise :

Saanvi : Who is Chandni?

Chandni smiling :

Chandni : Mother, you sit here, I will tell you who is.

Chandni gets up from the chair and makes Saanvi sit on the chair. And happily introduces :

Chandni : This is Reyansh, and Reyansh is my mother.

Reyansh greets Saanvi. Saanvi also greets him.

Chandni : We met in Budapest, or you can say we met on the plane.

Saanvi smiles looking at Reyansh and says:

Saanvi : How handsome isn't it!

Chandni : I know.

Saanvi : Do you have a girlfriend?

Chandni to Reyansh :

Chandni : Reyansh we talk later, okay bye.

Reyansh : Bye.

Video call cut.

Saanvi : Chandni I was talking, why did you cut the call?

Chandni : Mother, he has a girlfriend.

Saanvi normally :

Saanvi : Ooh nice.

Chandni : don'

The Dark Moon

t you want to ask, who is she?

Saanvi : Who....?

>Chandni blushes with a smile. Saanvi surprisingly :

Saanvi : You....

Chandni : Yes Mom.

>Saanvi happily hugs her and says:

Saanvi : I am so happy for you.

Chandni : thank you, Mom.

>Saanvi makes Chandni sit on the bed and keeps looking at her smiling, Chandni gets confused and asks :

Chandni : Why are you looking like this?

Saanvi : I see how beautiful the moon looks even with a smile.

>Chandni smiling :

Chandni : You know Mom, I met a woman over there, Sameera, she is just like me, just like me, She explained to me that the moon is not beautiful because it is the moon, He is beautiful because he comes out in the dark of night, I don't want to be a beautiful moon, I have accepted myself as I am.

>There are tears in Saanvi's eyes, she cries from Chandni with folded hands and says :

Saanvi : Forgive us.

>She gets nervous seeing Saanvi crying.

Chandni : Mother why are you apologizing?

Saanvi : Because of this racism, we have given you a lot of trouble, you have always said bad things.

Chandni smiles wiping Saanvi's tears and says :

Chandni : Mother forget everything, because of tomorrow, we will spoil us tomorrow only, by combining the bad picture of yesterday, we make a new picture.

Smiling Saanvi :

Saanvi : You have really changed.

Chandni : It was necessary to change, otherwise people in this world do not let them live.

He got up from the bed and walked towards the window :

Chandni : There would have been a lot of difference between living life and understanding life, I understood this very late but not anymore, Now I will not allow myself to hurt anyone, I just need you guys.

Saanvi is surprised :

Saanvi : What are you going to do?

Chandni sees Saanvi smiling and tells her everything. Hearing all this, Saanvi gives her courage :

Saanvi : You just walk, we're after you.

And hugs her.

Chandni : thank you, mom.

Next day :

The Dark Moon

> Chandni and Chhaiya are thinking of the name of the channel sitting in the hall at Chhaiya's house.

Chhaiya : Dude, this is a great job, what should be the name of the channel?

Chandni : I think my name should be Chandni.

Chhaiya : But you are reporting, you want to reach new people around the world.

Chandni : Not only news, I can also upload informative videos.

Chhaiya : Hmm. , Okay, then done, your YouTube channel name is Chandni.

> Both become happy.
>
> When Aarav comes from his office :

Aarav : Hello girls, what is happening?

Chhaiya : Chandni's channel was named Done.

Aarav : So what's the name?

Chandni : Chandni.

Aarav : This to was placed 24 years back.

Chandni : shut up.

> Aarav starts smiling. From Chhaiya Aarav :

Chhaiya : You get fresh, then eat dinner together.

Aarav : Someone else is about to come.

> Chhaiya in one breath :

Chhaiya : Who? And you told me why not, if a guest comes, then you have to tell, you....

Aarav : Relax dude, Reyansh Is coming, you have just climbed.

Chandni   : Reyansh is coming!

    Chhaiya is angry :

Chhaiya : He is his first visit here, and when did you invite him? You are really crazy.

    Aarav nervously looks at the moonlight, Chandni is very comfortable with him:

Chandni : Don't look at me, you really are.

Aarav   : What?

Chandni : Crazy, you're really crazy.

    Both run towards the kitchen.

Aarav   : Man what has happened?

Aarav himself in voice :

Aarav   : These women also do not understand, if someone comes then why they become so hyper.

    Chhaiya came out in anger to Aarav:

Chhaiya : If you are done talking to yourself, then get fresh.

    And goes away. Aarav to himself in a low voice:

Aarav   : How angry are you?

    Shouting from Chhaya Kitchen:

Chhaya : You didn't go?

    Shouting out to Aarav Dar:

Aarav   : I am going

    Aarav runs to his room.

    Dinner time :

The Dark Moon

From Chhaiya Reyansh :

Chhaiya : I would have known that you are going, so many more things would have happened.

Reyansh in sign language :

Reyansh : it's okay.

Chhaya looks at Aarav angrily.

Rao gets nervous seeing Chhaiya, and says to Chandni :

Aarav : Chandni?

Chandni : yes?

Aarav : So you thought how would you start your business?

Chandni : of course, main ne aur Chhaiya ne puri planning kar li hai, hum mere room ko hi Studio banayenge, humme bas ek ache camera ki zaroorat hai, uske liye kal hum mall jayenge, baaki ka kaam hum thode din baad shuru karenge.

Everyone enjoys dinner :

A few days later. Chandni's room is now her studio along with her room.

Those people made a video on recent news and are going to upload it on their YouTube channel. Both are sitting on the bed with laptops, Chandni is very nervous, Chhaiya to Chandni :

Chhaiya : Come on, I am done editing, now you upload it.

Chandni : I...

Chhaiya : nope me, of course, you, Quickly upload now and start your new journey.

> Chandni was very nervous, her hands started trembling and sweating, Chhaiya held her hand and engorged her with her eyes, Chandni holds Chaiyya tightly and says :

Chandni : Will you be with me on this new journey?

Chhaiya : of course.

Chandni : So, let's start this journey together.

> Both smile and upload the video. Hug each other.

> This thing takes a few days. One night, Viraj used to post comments on Chandni's YouTube channel, there are 5 comments, which would have 2 good and 3 bad comments. Seeing Viraj, Saanvi asks him:

Saanvi : What happened? You seem tense.

Viraj : Did you read the comments on Chandni's video?

Saanvi : No, why? Comments are not good?

Viraj : There are good and bad too, I come to meet Chandni.

> There are good and bad too, I come to meet Chandni :

Chandni : I wish my work helps people.

> Chandni gets very sad after reading the comments on her phone.

> At the same time, Viraj knocks on her room.

The Dark Moon

Viraj : Come in?

Chandni : Dad come.

> Viraj also sits on the Rakhi chair next to Chandni.

Viraj : What are you doing?

> Viraj saw the comments on his phone.

Viraj : Were you getting comments?

> Chandni gets sad. Viraj engrossing her:

Viraj : Son you did a great job in that video.

Chandni : thank you dad.

Viraj : I know, you are sad after reading these negative comments, but look at that also there are 2 good comments on it, who are appreciating your work.

Chandni : But 3 people are not doing evil to my work, they are calling me bad.

> Viraj lays his hand on Chandni's head:

Viraj : oh my dear, You leave these 3 comments and pay attention to this 2 comment, always remember one thing, This journey is like a rose flower, where a beautiful flower also has thorns, and you will have to bear that thing too, But you just have to pay attention to the fragrance of that flower.

> Chandni Nervously :

Chandni : I know, the journey I am on is going to be very difficult for me, but will I be able to do all this?

Kahkashan Zaid

Viraj : Surely, why did God choose you for this journey? Because you are capable of this, the one above us knows more than we do. You can and will do this, we all are not with you behind you.

Chandni smiles and hugs her dad.

Chandni : Thank you dad.

Chandni would make and upload videos. She would get sad after reading negative comments again and again, but everyone used to meet her and arrange. Most of his videos were of his teenage years, many people would appreciate his work and many people would make fun of his complexion. Ananya too sees Chandni's video and smiles.

It's been 3 years since this. Chandni is waiting for Reyansh sitting on the beach. Reyansh comes, and Chandni is furious :

Chandni : Where were you Reyansh, I have been waiting for you the for last 1 hour.

Reyansh makes an innocent appearance and says :

Reyansh : sorry.

Chandni : This is your issue, say sorry by making an innocent appearance and ending the talk, who should get angry on this appearance?

At the same time a 14-year-old child comes there, Suraj.

The Dark Moon

Suraj : You are Chandni, aren't you?

Chandni gets nervous.

Chandni : Yes I am Chandni, who are you?

Suraj : I am a subscriber.

Chandni gets happy.

Suraj : My name is Suraj, I like your videos very much, how well you explain things, I always wait for your videos, whenever anything is happening, I do not go anywhere, I just wait when you will tell us the whole truth.

Tears come to Chandni's eyes after hearing this, she smiles and looks at Reyansh.

At the same time Suraj's mother, Neha comes there staring at Chandni. To his mother in Suraj Excitement :

Suraj : mom see Chandni.

Chandni and Reyansh stand up.

Neha : Are you, YouTube Chandni?

Chandni : Yes.

Neha : You are doing a great job, every person in our house has subscribed to you, people like you are lacking in this country, jo bina jhoot aur bina darr ke sach bolte hai, Those who speak the truth without lies and without fear, our coming generation is getting a lot of benefit from your truth.

Chandni : You are appreciating our work for a lot of Shukriya.

Neha : Can we take a picture with you?

Neha gives her phone to Reyansh.

Neha : Please click our photo!

Chandni sees Reyansh smiling, and Reyansh happily clicks their pictures. after the picture is clicked.

Neha : You are very good, and please keep making videos like this, thank you.

Chandni : thank you.

Suraj : bye.

Chandni : bye.

And both leave from there. Chandni happily hugs Reyansh and starts crying. Reyansh walks his hand on his head with great love.

Chandni tells all this to Chhaiya in her studio, Chhaiya happily hugs her and says:

Chhaiya : This is a great achievement for you lost.

Chandni : There is no achievement for me.

Chhaiya : So, what is it for?

Chandni : This achievement is not only mine, it is ours, this achievement is ours, it belongs to everyone, who supports the truth, now we have to work with better people.

Chhaiya : Let it all happen.

A few days later. In the evening, Chhaiya gets tired of working, she takes the rings. Chandni to Chhaiya :

Chandni : What happened, are you tired?

The Dark Moon

Chhaiya : Yes man, now I should go home, and before that I have to go to the market to get some stuff.

Chandni : I also go along, get tired of sitting in this same room, go to the market, so maybe the mind becomes fresh.

Chhaiya : OK, let's go, let's go.

Both leave the room and come downstairs. From Saanvi :

Saanvi : Where are you two going?

Chandni : We are going to the market and then Chhaiya went to her house from there.

Saanvi : Alright.

Both leave the house. Divya sees Chandni.

Chandni : Hello Auntie! how are you

Divya : I'm fine, where are you two going?

Chandni : We are going to the market.

Divya : Well, please take some vegetables for me too.

Chandni and Chhaiya start seeing each other's face. Divya to Chandni :

Divya : Don't have to bring much, wait both of you, I will bring money and list.

Chandni : That aunt is not too much and the list is also ready.

Divya : Shut up, I'll come.

Chandni : Okay but hurry up.

Divya : Yes, yes.

~ 117 ~

Kahkashan Zaid

    Divya goes inside the house. Both are waiting for him outside. Both get tired while waiting :

Chhaiya : Where is Auntie left?

Chandni shouting out loud :

Chandni : Auntie we are going.

Divya comes out running :

Divya : coming....., today's children do not even have patience, take this list and money, and don't forget anything, today Bhanu has not come, only you will drive the market back.

Chandni : okay, Here I come.

    By taking all the belongings of both, it is done by Chandni Chhaiya :

Chandni : Alright, you get out now and I'll go home.

    Seeing more stuff in Chhaiya's hand, Chhaiya says :

Chhaiya : You have a lot of stuff in your hand, let me leave you home and go back to my house.

Chandni : No, there is no need for this, you will be very late.

Chhaiya : Chandni but.....

Chandni : But nothing, you go home, I will also go.

    Chandni stops the auto for Chhaiya and sits with him. Concern for Chandni:

Chhaiya : Chandni mian abhi bhi keh rahi hoon.

    I am still saying in the moonlight.

    Chandni to Auto man :

~ 118 ~

The Dark Moon

Chandni : Brother, take it to his house directly.

Auto man took his auto :

From Herself till Chandni after the departure of Chhaiya :

Chandni : Very heavy hai man, Divya aunty, I will tell you.

While Chandni is walking towards the house, a crowd of people can be seen from afar.

Chandni : Why is there so much crowd here?

She goes to that crowd, and sees that a dog is lying dead, she gets sad seeing him.

Chandni listens to people's words :

Girl : It's a pet dog, don't know who left his stomach to kill.

Chandni gets shocked to hear this.

Every mom : How do you know it's a pet dog?

Girl : This evening is also with my friend, and I only saw him yesterday.

Every Mother : Isn't he having a stomach?

Girl : No Mom, it's been a week now, buy from him.

Seeing the condition of that dog, everyone is feeling sorry for that dog, and the smell is also coming.

Woman : I don't know how people are animals, these humans bring dogs for their own purposes, and when they are bored, they do not take care of them, In the same way, the pet leaves the dog on the way, the pet is not able to survive on the way and die, the human being is as cruel as the human being.

Chandni is listening to all this and is looking at that dog.

She is coming home thinking about that dog, she is just moving towards her house, Divya is making noise after seeing Chandni.

Divya : Chandni! Chandni! What has happened to Her?

Chandni is going towards her house, she does not hear Divya's voice.

When Chandni comes home, Saanvi sees more stuff in her hand and asks her :

Saanvi : Chandni! Whose stuff is this, I had not ordered anything!

Chandni quietly goes to her room after keeping things on the table. Saanvi Confusingly :

Saanvi : What happened to her?

Just then Divya comes to Saanvi:

Divya : Saanvi! What happened to Chandni?
Saanvi : Don't know? And don't know why it has brought so much stuff.
Divya : I ordered this from Chandni.
Saanvi : Oh.
Divya : Will you go to the room?
Saanvi : Let's see what happened.

The Dark Moon

Divya : Come on, come on.

> Both come to his room.
>
> Both open the door of his room. Chandni is doing something on her laptop. Saanvi and Divya to each other :

Divya : What happened with this, it was okay to go!

Saanvi : I don't know what would have happened!

> Chandni hears the whispers of both and says to both :

Chandni : You both come in.

> Both come inside. From Saanvi Chandni:

Chandni : What happened?

> Divya and her laptop see a file of Pet Dogs Abandoned :

Divya : And what is this? Why are you reading about these dogs?

Chandni : First of all, both of you sit down.

> Both sit, Chandni told both of them about the dog's accident.
>
> After hearing all, all three of them feel sorry. Chandni showing on laptop :

Chandni : See, it's not just dogs, cats, rabbits, and many other animals that are adopted, and financial issues, because of boredom, And because of not giving time, he is left on the way, Street animals do survive because they have a habit but pets are difficult to survive and after a few weeks they die on the way,

How bad do these giants do with these senseless animals.

And she gets very upset. Divya and Saanvi start looking at each other, Divya stands up to him and puts his hand on his head, and says with great love :

Divya : Look, Chandni, don't put yourself under stress with all these things, yes, I agree, There are some people who adopt pets to overcome their loneliness, And for some reason, they leave them to die on the way, but now we all can't tell them to go to them, not why did you do this, Because there is no such one, don't know how many people are there, you can't explain everything to everyone, can you?

The idea came to Chandni :

Chandni : Can do it.

Saanvi and Divya start looking at each other:

Saanvi : How?

Chandni smiles thinking and says :

Chandni : we can do it.

Next day :

Chhaiya comes to Chandni's room, and as soon as she comes, she shows Chandni the viral video of that pet dog :

Chhaiya : Seeing this moonlight, what is tomorrow?

By watching Chandni's video:

Chandni : Our next video is on this.

The Dark Moon

Chandni tells him everything and asks him to work.

A few days later Chandni uploads her video.

Suraj is using the phone, and Neha is sitting on the sofa reading books.

Suraj : Mother! Chandni's new video has arrived.

Neha : Okay... What is the title?

Suraj : stop abandoning pets.

Neha : Come let's see together.

After a lot of people got the notification, those people started watching the video.

Video starts :

Chandni : Hello friends. Recently a video went viral.

The video of that dog is shown in the video.

Chandni : This pet dog was taken away by its owner, and left it alone on the way, we all know, What is the difference between street dogs and pet dogs, street dogs make arrangements for everything they eat and sleep, When a pet dog is completely different from it, its owner feeds it, feeds it, bathes it, overall it depends on a person, And we humans leave such dogs alone on the way so…….., (Deep Breath) So it becomes difficult for them to live and they die within a few days.

Chandni got upset and says :

Chandni : I have to say with great regret that we humans are doing this too wild animals like human beings, This is not just a case, don't know how many places such cases would be, and not only happens with dogs, This happens with every animal that adopts animals and then after getting bored or Due to financial issues, he leaves her alone to die on the way, sometimes I think, Whether the animal is it or we, we humans, do not disloyal to, Now tell me what is its solution? There is a solution in my opinion...., that is the pet house from which we adopt the pets. What if we donate the same pet later in the same pet house?

Everyone gets confused after hearing this. Surprised to hear this exclusive :

Anonymous : What is she saying?

Chandni smiling :

Chandni : You all must be wondering what she is talking about! I try to explain my point to you. The penthouse from which you have bought the pet, if you get bored with your stomach going forward, then you donate the same pet to the same pet house, Due to which that stomach will not be harmed and your money will also be recovered, now you must be thinking, what is the use of us in this, There is no advantage in this that you leave that stomach on the way to kill, when we go for our blood donation, So in that only thinks about the life of the person in front, here also the same thing has to be done, It is

The Dark Moon

better to leave to kill that pet than to donate it in the same pet house, the rest of you understand, I join hands in front, do not get rid of them on the way to kill the pets, what is your opinion on this matter, please share in the comment box.

Video ends.

Seeing this video, a lot of people appreciated the talk of Chandni :

Punjabi uncle :

Uncle : The girl has spoken very well.

Muslim Aunty :

Aunt : This thinking of Chandni may change the thinking of people on this matter.

But some people also said very bad things.

Mind : The black huts are thinking of saving the dogs.

And starts laughing.

Woman : Such people do not know why they are famous, all acting is on, and they do anything to be famous.

Chandni started paying attention to the positive comments and would have been very happy. Reyansh and Chandni hugging each other while sitting on the beach:

Chandni : I wish this thought of mine reaches the people, and instead of leaving their pets on the way, people donate them in the penthouse itself, do you think this will work?

Reyansh : Yes.

And kisses him on the forehead.

Chandni hugs him again.

4 years later.

Book launch Event Interview :

Anchor : I am personally very happy to have our author today, because what they did is wonderful work, and we all pray that he continues to do more work like this, please welcome and give a big appliance. Chandni.....

When the moonlight comes, everyone stands up, seeing this, Saanvi and Viraj have tears in their eyes, there are also Reyansh, Aarav, Chhaiya, and Divya. Everyone is standing and clapping for him.

Chandni tells everyone standing on the stage :

Chandni : thank you guys, thank you, please have a seat.

Everybody sits down :

Anchor : hello Chandni, welcome and please have a seat.

Chandni : thank you.

Anchor : People are very excited to know your story.

Chandni : And I want to tell you, that's why I have written a book 'The Dark Moon.'

Anchor : But we want to hear something from your tongue.

The Dark Moon

Chandni : Like?

Anchor : Like, why do you want to reach your story to the people?

Chandni : As you all know, I'm black, but this confident person, this journey of calling himself black was very difficult, Do you know when children are born, the first question is whether it is a boy or a girl? If there is a girl, then the second question is whether she is black or fair, I don't know why people care whether the girl is black or fair, And those same people who are black themselves are more sorry, we have been taught the difference between black and white since childhood, It is these societies that teach children the difference in color, white girls are beautiful and black girls are unlucky, But the place where I am today is a black girl, not a white one, and I can say Proudly that I am a black Woman.

Everyone is clapping for Chandni on this point.

Anchor : You are an individual journalist, don't you believe in TV news channels?

Chandni : Are you sure?

Anchor : 50 percent.

Chandni : 60 percent.

Anchor : Then why did you choose the path of individual journalism?

~ 127 ~

Kahkashan Zaid

Chandni : Firstly, I love to know things by myself, and secondly, If TV news channels stop showing Hindu-Muslim conflicts in our country, people will pay attention to something else.

Anchor : Good answer, what is the biggest thing you have learned in your life?

Chandni : The biggest thing I have learned in my life is that........, you cannot change society.

Anchor : So what needs to be changed?

Chandni : I speak for myself, my own thinking, I speak for myself, I have been hearing one thing since childhood, that I am black, And I guess these things have never been changedin society, but what can we change? That is by accepting myself, my own thinking, and this thing I have learned from my life.

Anchor : The last question.

Chandni : Yes.

Anchor : Which character is there in your book that is with you from the beginning of the book till the end of the book?

Chandni : Where I am today in my life is only because of her, there was no one with me then she came into my life, For some reason I removed her from me but she did not get away from me, she is the most beautiful character of my life, My Best friend Chhaiya.

Chandni looks at him and gives a big smile, Chhaiya has tears in her eyes and a smile on her lips.

The Dark Moon

Everyone was clipping.

Chandni goes to Chhaiya and brings her on stage, together they launch Chandni's book. There is a picture of both Chhaiya and Chandni on that book cover.

Seeing this, Chhaya hugs Chandni.

Sab Chandni ki signature book ke liye line se khade ho jaate hai. At the same time, someone gives their CV in Her hand. Chandni sees Her face, Ananya to Chandni:

Ananya : Got a job?

Both start laughing and hug each other.

Chandni : Why not man?

After some time:

Chandni and Reyansh get married, full white theme In their marriage, Chhaiya also has her baby boy in her hand, who is just like Chhaiya.

A year later, Chandni delivers, she has a black girl, Chandni smiles at her.

Chandni : She is black.

And kisses him on her forehead. Reyansh kisses both of them on their foreheads.

If dark colour is shortcoming in humans, then it is the most beautiful shortcoming in humans.

Kahkashan Zaid

Previous Book

Printed in the USA
CPSIA information can be obtained
at www.ICGtesting.com
LVHW052232290324
775848LV00004B/315